THE SUPERIOR PERSON'S

GUIDE TO

EVERYDAY IRRITATIONS

BY

RUSS LINDWAY

Illustrated by PAUL MICHAEL DAVIES

CCC PUBLICATIONS • LOS ANGELES

Published by

CCC Publications
20306 Tau Place
Chatsworth, CA 91311

Copyright © 1990 Russ Lindway

Manufactured in the United States of America

Cover design © 1990 CCC Publications

Illustrations © 1990 Russ Lindway

Original cover concept/art & interior art
by Paul Michael Davies

Cover Color/art by Suzanne Carroll Feinsinger

Cover Production by The Creative Place

ISBN: 0-918259-23-1

If your local U.S. bookstore is out of stock, copies of this book may be obtained by mailing check or money order for $4.95 per book (plus $1.50 to cover sales tax, postage and handling) to: CCC Publications; 20306 Tau Place; Chatsworth, CA 91311.

Pre-publication edition — 2/90

ACKNOWLEDGEMENTS

Special thanks go to Lee and Russ Senior for being ultra-Superior Parents, and to Karen Poltrone and Diane Krall for being Superior Siblings who inflicted their respective senses of humor on me at a very early age. Big-time appreciation goes to Mike Centanni, ESQ! for patiently explaining all that legal stuff to me. To Bob Tetzloff, who laughs at my ideas no matter how bad they are, and to Les Szekely, who influences me by being unceasingly creative, thanks for being the pals of a lifetime. Much gratitude goes to Mark Chutick for the opportunity to be published, and to Cliff Carle for the supreme editorial guidance.

Finally, a big "thank you" to D.A.B. for absolutely nothing.

This book and all that led up to it is for Jean, who the term "Superior" only begins to describe.

INTRODUCTION

Stomach churning ... mind racing ... heart rate increasing ... fists clenching ...

These are sure signs of mental and/or emotional irritation. Everybody gets irritated. Even seemingly easy-going, even-tempered folk get P.O.'d once in a while.

There are some people, though, who are so acutely aware of the environment, so ultra-sensitive to what is going on around them, that they can't help but be irritated by the slightest deviation from comfort, convenience or common sense. These sensitive, aware individuals become irritated *very* frequently. These sensitive, aware individuals are SPs ... Superior Persons.

This book is for all the Superior People in the world. Oh sure, everyone is *created* equal, but what happens after that is each person's own doing. As the saying goes, some people *are* more equal than others.

Yes, Superior People *do* exist. They comprise every race, creed, color, religion, age, sex and political affiliation. You're reading this, so *you're* probably one of them. Hooray for you. If you're unsure as to your Superior Status, this book will allow you to make that determination, long before you're finished with it.

It must be understood that being Superior is radically different from having a superiority *complex*. People who blatantly act like they're *better* than everyone else have a superiority complex ... people who think they're always *right* have a superiority complex. They are also snobs.

True Superiors know *when* they are right and, more importantly, *never* get obnoxious about it when they are. However, since they always know *when* they're right, SPs are easily bothered by the most trivial imperfections in technology and human nature. The fact that they're irritated almost constantly does *not* mean they're right or better or smarter (although, let's face it, it *could* mean that). These individuals are simply more closely in touch with their own emotions and the outside world than are most people. And *that* is what makes them Superior.

By means of comparison and assimilation, you will be able to recognize your own personal irritations — perhaps become aware of some you never knew you had and take pride in being a Superior Person.

THE CATEGORIES

Anything that can cause people irritation can be categorized. The following are the fifteen most common categories:

It should be stated here that all these categories somehow relate to social situations. And naturally, social situations involve people. Ergo, a majority of these irritations come from human beings. However, while certain human stereotypes are alluded to in this book, no race or class of people is intentionally demeaned, put down or ridiculed. People who *do* certain things are studied here, not people who *are* certain things.

Each item is accompanied by a numerical Irritation Quotient. This reading gives you an idea of how intensely a given irritation affects the average Superior Person:

.5 - 3.0 is a Mild Distraction.

3.5 - 6.0 is a Fairly Strong Annoyance.

6.5 - 9.5 is a Full-Fledged Vexation.

10.0 is when all your fingernails are simultaneously bent back and your tongue is stuck to dry ice. (Or something approximating that combined sensation.)

What follows then, are the everyday situations which true SPs will find irritating. So please, read ... let off a little steam ... and most of all, enjoy.

vi

CATEGORY #1:
TELEVISION
(The Half-Vast Wasteland)

It's fitting to begin this critical study of human nature with a formidable man-made force in popular culture: television. This revolutionary concept in mass communication — or "Boob Tube" — exists in nearly every American's life every day of the year. It's only natural that it would create its own special source of annoyance.

As you'll see, these irritations stem from the actual television sets themselves, as well as the phenomena the technology has spawned.

SPECIAL NEWS BULLETINS WHICH PRE-EMPT THE MOST CRUCIAL PART OF A PROGRAM YOU ARE WATCHING.

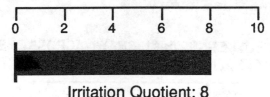

0   2   4   6   8   10

Irritation Quotient: 8

This is one of the most maddening fist-clenchers in the entire category. Everyone knows Superior People don't give a damn about the subjects of emergency news reports. "World

War III?? Who cares?? Who's sleeping with who on *thirtysomething*, that's what *we* want to know!"

The news flash will invariably interrupt your show right before the murderer is revealed, or during the climactic chase sequence, or else it will end and return to your show during the loudest laughter portion of the entire story. You can't figure out what happened because none of the actors say anything while the studio audience is rolling in the aisles.

And don't you love it when you'd swear the news announcer *knows* you care more about your program than his report? He feels obligated to tell you, "The following is a special news bulletin" and that "the preceding was a special news bulletin" and you should "stay tuned for further special news bulletins" all in a slow, dramatic delivery which conveniently wraps up just in time to return to a commercial.

By the way, the irritation that results from this occurrence is a bit more powerful if you happen to be taping the program for permanent inclusion in your home video library.

WEATHER BULLETINS WHICH CRAWL ACROSS THE BOTTOM OF THE TV SCREEN.

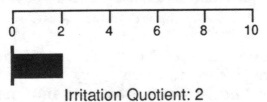

Irritation Quotient: 2

As if this intrusion isn't bad enough, it's usually preceded by a grating ***BEEP! BEEP! BEEP!***

2

which drowns out important program dialogue. Then, to beat a dead horse, the TV station feels the need to run the warning *twice* for all the illiterates at home who couldn't get it all the first time.

A POWER FAILURE THAT OCCURS WHILE YOU'RE WATCHING A PROGRAM.

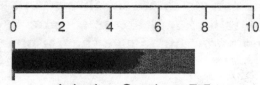

Irritation Quotient: 7.5

Power failures by themselves are exasperating. When your attention is glued to the set and all goes black, that's a double-whammy. But wouldn't it be great if the action on the show you were watching went dead, too, and when the power came back on, the show resumed where it left off? Dream on!

STAYING UP LATE TO WATCH A PROGRAM YOU'VE WAITED ALL WEEK FOR, ONLY TO SEE AN UNANNOUNCED RERUN OF *WILD KINGDOM* **INSTEAD.**

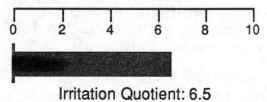

Irritation Quotient: 6.5

This actually happens to Superiors quite often (not always with *Wild Kingdom* of course, but you get the idea).

You know the scenario: There's a late-night program in your local listing which you really want to see and you missed it the first 18 times it was on. You wait all week, manage to prop your eyelids open until 2 a.m., and as your reward you see the opening credits to a show which you immediately know is *not* the one you rearranged your life for.

All you can do is curse, throw your bedroom slipper (or table lamp) at the set and vow to call the station tomorrow to give them a piece of your mind.

DISCOVERING A FAVORITE SHOW OF YOURS FROM LAST SEASON HAS BEEN CANCELLED.

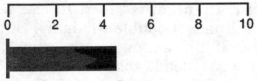

Irritation Quotient: 4.5

Like discovering your favorite amusement park ride was torn down without your permission, finding out a TV program you loved last year is now gone from the new fall schedule is indeed a sad occasion. Invariably, sad gives way to mad, and you then threaten to start a letter-writing campaign to save the show.

Hey, why not? It worked for *Star Trek* and *Cagney and Lacey*.

GETTING COMFORTABLE ON THE COUCH TO WATCH TV, ONLY TO DISCOVER THE REMOTE CONTROL IS ON TOP OF THE SET ON THE OTHER SIDE OF THE ROOM.

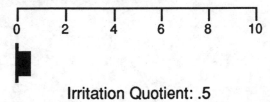

Irritation Quotient: .5

A minor annoyance which is easily remedied. Still, you can't help but ask yourself who the hell put the remote *on top* of the TV. The answer is — four times out of five — *you* did.

***TECHNICAL DIFFICULTIES* WHICH "CONVENIENTLY" STRIKE DURING YOUR FAVORITE SHOW.**

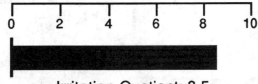

Irritation Quotient: 8.5

There must be one technician at each and every station in America whose sole function is to interrupt the signal that goes into your television antenna at given times, replacing it with a "please stand by" slide which features a cutesy illustration of a confused man leaning his head through a broken TV screen.

A more appropriate visual would be to have an SP's foot making contact with the confused man's rear end.

SETTING YOUR VCR TO RECORD A ONCE-IN-A-LIFETIME PROGRAM, THEN COMING HOME TO REALIZE YOU DID EVERYTHING BUT SELECT THE CORRECT CHANNEL.

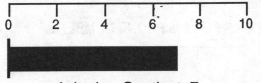

Irritation Quotient: 7

VCRs are an offshoot of television which demonstrate their own growing irritation potential. This is a prime example, even though forgetting to set the channel or failing to select AM instead of PM isn't the machine's fault. However, all Superiors know the importance of blaming inanimate objects for their own absent-mindedness.

This particular one eats away at your gut a little more than it should because the irritation is delayed until a later time when your expectation that the machine recorded flawlessly is very high.

GETTING LESS THAN PERFECT RECEPTION FROM YOUR EXPENSIVE CABLE TELEVISION SYSTEM.

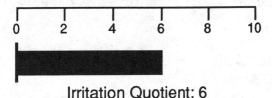

Irritation Quotient: 6

You're paying big bucks for great reception that allegedly only cable TV can give you. So when your picture looks like someone is running an electric knife in your kitchen, it's time to get mad, cancel your cable subscription and renew your *Playboy* subscription. It's available 24 hours a day, the pictures are always sharp, and you can skip past the ads without a remote.

COMMERCIALS FOR 976 PHONE NUMBERS.

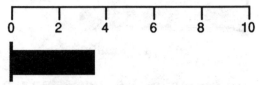

Irritation Quotient: 3.5

Teen talk. Party-Line. Uncle Barfy's Scary Stories. Debbie Gibson's beauty hints. DJ Jazzy Jeff and the Fresh Prince's rap music theory.

SPs are firm believers that the tolls for dialing 976 numbers aren't high *enough.* Schleps who call these time-wasters should pay hundreds of dollars, at least — per call.

The commercials for 976 numbers, however, are inflicted daily on people who wouldn't dream of calling them, and these spots are so incredibly bad, many a television screen has undoubtedly been bashed in because of what they do to human nerves.

TV PROGRAMS WHICH ARE REALLY EXTENDED COMMERCIALS.

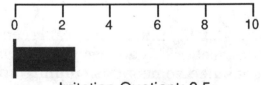

Irritation Quotient: 2.5

Thirty-minute programs which detail subjects like the Amazing Brussels Hair Formula or Getting Rich in One Hard Lesson are moderately vexing, mostly because the TV stations that air these "extended commercials" obviously have little regard for the audience they now have, or would like to have in the future.

PEOPLE WHO WOULD RATHER DIE THAN MISS "MY SOAP."

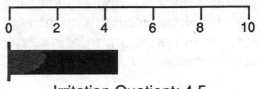

Irritation Quotient: 4.5

What this condition sadly translates to is this: These individuals admit that the lives of fictitious, one-dimensional characters are more exciting than their own.

What's really sad is, they're probably right.

BLACK-AND-WHITE MOVIES WHICH HAVE BEEN COLORIZED.

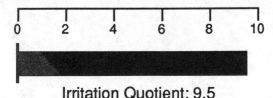

Irritation Quotient: 9.5

A stormy brouhaha is being waged between money-grubbing TV executives and film makers, critics and buffs over whether black-and-white movies should be tampered with by colorizing them through computer technology.

9

SPs are usually purists in regard to this issue: How it was made is how it should stay.

Can you imagine seeing *The Wizard of Oz* with the Kansas scenes in color? They might even change the Oz scenes to black-and-white! After all, they're only interested in change. The concept of "artistic integrity" is obviously beyond their grasp.

* * *

Now, please stand by, don't touch that dial, and get ready to switch mediums. Who says you need a television image to entertain, inform ... and irritate? Sound can accomplish these things all by itself ...

CATEGORY #2:
RADIO
(Polluting the Airwaves)

In your car, in your office, in almost every room of your home ... the radio is ever-present in your life, maybe even more so than TV sets.

The voices and sounds that come out of radios are often taken for granted, but there are some notable irritations that beg not to be ignored. Whether you're tuned to AM or FM, your innocent little radio can be quite bothersome ... for instance ...

RADIO PERSONALITIES WHO RIP OFF JOKES THEY HEARD ON TV THE NIGHT BEFORE.

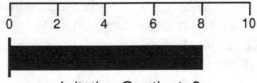

Irritation Quotient: 8

Attack of the Small-Minded Leeches!

These deejays are the ones who do their zany AM-type schtick every day of the week, so are in constant need of new material. The hitch is, they can't possibly dream up that much stuff on their own and are too cheap to hire writers — so they appropriate jokes they hear on the tube, make them out as their own and hope none of their listeners watched the show they stole them from.

The most annoying thing about this practice is hearing these jocks trying to convince the audience it's all original material. They'll slip it into normal conversation with the newsman, play some uproarious laugh-track, adopt a smug demeanor and everyone thinks they're so-o-o-o-o funny. They don't even give the TV program or the comedian who actually thought up the line any credit!

Credit these third-rate losers with the title of "Professional Amateur."

MORNING SHOWS WHICH UTILIZE 5 OR MORE WACKY "PERSONALITIES."

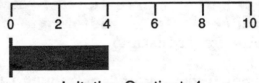

Irritation Quotient: 4

Remember when pop/rock radio used to play music in the morning? On the way to work you could roll down the windows and crank up the tunes, or if you decided to sing along, you'd roll *up* the windows and crank up the tunes.

Not so anymore. Now you've got "wake-up shows" featuring a half-dozen or more would-be comedians and self-proclaimed "personalities" crammed together in the same studio bombarding you with endless yakking, stupid stolen jokes and forced laughter from the ones who don't happen to be talking at that moment.

Annoying morning programs like this make a tape player in your car all that more valuable.

DISC JOCKEYS WHO TALK OVER THE WORDS TO A SONG.

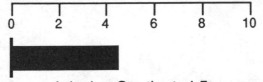

Irritation Quotient: 4.5

A good Top-40 jock prides himself on the fact that he can ad lib over the musical intro to a song and finish talking a split-second before the singing starts. That's called "being tight."

An inferior jock is one who continually mistimes his spiel or who just plain doesn't know when to shut up, and therefore steps on the vocals. That's called "being a schmuck who should be canned and never allowed to work in this town again — ever!"

DISC JOCKEYS WHO MISPRONOUNCE SINGERS' NAMES OR MISREAD SONG TITLES.

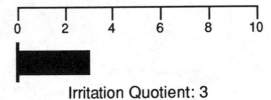

Irritation Quotient: 3

These are people who are supposed to be professionals and, like all professionals, are supposed to know what the hell they're talking about. So, when a jock announces "The Lady in Red" by Chris De Burgh as "The *Woman* in Red" or "The Boys of Summer" by Don *Henry* instead of Don *Henley*, one wonders how this "talent" keeps his job when there are literate, aware people who could perform so much better ... like you, for instance.

WAITING IN VAIN FOR THE DEEJAY TO ANNOUNCE WHO SINGS A SONG YOU JUST HEARD.

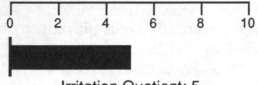

Irritation Quotient: 5

What a frustrating waste of time this is! You hear a song you know, but for the life of you, you cannot remember who sings it. You abandon your immediate plans in order to hang by the radio speaker in hopes of hearing the deejay announce who it was.

Naturally, no such announcement comes, you end up being late for work, you are subsequently fired and end up being a street person ... all as a result of that thoughtless jock.

DISC JOCKEYS WHO PRETEND A SONG IS "BY REQUEST."

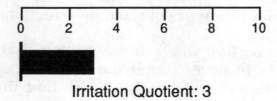

Irritation Quotient: 3

15

Since most pop radio these days comes across the airwaves in a homogenized "hits" format, it becomes obvious to any remotely observant listener that deejays have a set list of boffo-smash songs to play.

So, when you hear a Top-40 jock start a record and announce that it's "by request," you immediately know he's lying. It's actually by *command* — the Program Director's command — because the record is part of the station's regular rotation and would have eventually been played anyway! Your duty then is to call the jock and angrily tell him not to give you any of this "by request" bull!

Be aware that your complaint won't change anything, but it does let you blow off steam.

RADIO STATIONS THAT CHANGE THEIR FORMATS OFTEN.

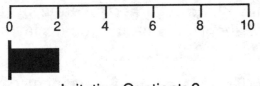

Irritation Quotient: 2

Stations that don't know if they want to play neo-classical reggae music or talk-radio barbershop concertos can be a bit distracting, especially to Superior People who are constantly on the lookout for new types of radio programming.

For, one day you'll find a station that makes you want to never touch the dial again, only to tune in one day a month later to find the entire on-air staff has been fired and replaced by an automated new age-metal service.

Back to your record collection.

SO-CALLED "CUTTING EDGE" ROCK STATIONS WHICH PLAY THE SAME SONGS AND ARTISTS EVERY OTHER "HIT" STATION PLAYS.

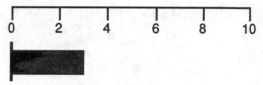

Irritation Quotient: 3

Give the people what they want, but call it something else to make them think it's cool and different. This type of station is a shepherd, its listeners sheep.

Be a wolf.

BEING THE TWENTY-FOURTH CALLER IN AN ALBUM GIVEAWAY IN WHICH THEY'RE LOOKING FOR THE TWENTY-*FIFTH* CALLER.

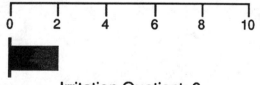

Irritation Quotient: 2

There's not much to lament about this one, which comes about because of pure luck (or lack thereof). However, it does create enough tension to push that pulse rate up a notch or two.

Easy solution: Stop calling and go out and *buy* the damn album.

* * *

In theory, Radio pleases the ears. What you've just read is how Radio sometimes <u>assaults</u> the ears. We now move ahead to another bit of technology which preys primarily on the sense of hearing ...

CATEGORY #3

THE TELEPHONE

(The Worst Kinds of Connections)

Can you imagine what life was like before telephones? You had to rely on the postal service and the Pony Express and smoke signals to communicate with loved ones and business associates, often waiting weeks or months to receive a reply.

You also had none of the following butt-burners, which have to do with the telephone itself and all the related inventions which came after it:

PEOPLE WHO SCREEN CALLS WITH THEIR ANSWERING MACHINE.

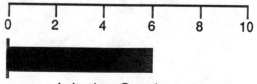

Irritation Quotient: 6

Who do these people think they are?

MARVIN? MARVIN, THIS IS YOUR MOTHER-IN-LAW!
PICK UP THE PHONE, MARVIN — I KNOW YOU'RE
THERE!! I NEED TO CONFIRM MY VISIT ... MARVIN?...

Most answering machines have speakers which allow the recipient of a call to hear the caller's voice. Some people use this feature for selfish ends, by leaving their answering machine on 24 hours a day, and listening for who is calling them before deciding whether to pick up the phone or not.

The unique thing about this irritation is that, as the caller, you never know if the person is really doing that, or if he simply isn't home. You only get irritated if you're actually in someone's home and you witness him screening a call.

A fun form of revenge is to dial their machine, say you're from "Dialing for Dollars," that you're sorry no one is home, and then abruptly hang up.

THE RUDENESS OF CALL-WAITING.

Irritation Quotient: 6.5

Ever been in the middle of a meaningful phone conversation when suddenly you hear an intrusive little clicking sound, as if a pony is galloping up your receiver cord?

That click is "Call Waiting," the amazing phone feature that tells the person who has it that he or she has another call coming in.

So what happens? The offender says, "Oh, just a minute," puts you abruptly on hold and leaves you hanging there, mid-syllable, often for minutes on end, while he attends to someone who he obviously considers *more important* than you.

This feature is understandable for small businesses. Residences having this feature on their phones should be against the law. The practice is rude, the "clicking" is rude, the whole concept is rude, rude, RUDE!

Next time you call someone with the Call-Waiting click, respond with your own sound effect: an air horn into the receiver.

PEOPLE WHO WON'T LEAVE A MESSAGE ON *YOUR* ANSWERING MACHINE.

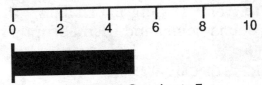

Irritation Quotient: 5

Some people can talk your ear off on the horn all night long. Yet amazingly, some of those same people claim they "just can't deal with talking to one of those contraptions," referring, of course, to answering machines. Do they think the C.I.A. is listening?

Consequently, you'll come home some days and eagerly play back three or four messages thinking, great, people are calling me! They really like me! ... only to find all of them consist of the sound of the receiver being clumsily slammed onto its cradle!

Why can't they leave a message? Phone fright? They don't even have to bother with verbs, or even phrases. All they have to say is, "Nancy. 555-5555," or "Bill."

But no, they're content with irritating you. And this is one of those rare two-part annoyances: You get irritated when you hear the hang-ups, and you get irritated all over again when you meet the culprit later and he says, "Oh, I tried calling you but you weren't home."

At this point you'd like to insert the receiver into his nearest orifice sideways.

TRYING TO CALL SOMEONE WHOSE LINE IS BUSY FOR HOURS ON END.

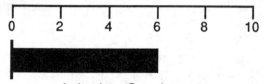

Irritation Quotient: 6

One of the most frustrating feelings in the world is trying to desperately get hold of someone by phone, and hearing that *baaahp! baaahp!* sound harshly attacking your ear drum every five minutes over a period of three hours.

Then, when you finally get through, your pal confesses, "Oh yeah, sorry, guess the receiver wasn't hung up straight."

PHONE SOLICITORS WHO ACCOST YOU WHEN YOU'RE WAITING FOR AN IMPORTANT CALL.

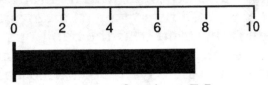

Irritation Quotient: 7.5

As sure as hell is a four-letter word, when you find yourself impatiently sitting by the phone, looking at your watch expecting an important call, and the phone finally rings, you pick up the receiver on the first ring, say "hello" and you hear ... "Hi, I'm Greg from Soakum and Droppum Insurance..."

This impeccable timing rarely fails, and all you can do is quickly blow the person off and go through the emotionally draining waiting process all over again. Of course, your important call probably got a busy signal while you were getting rid of the turkey.

PHONE SOLICITORS WHO TRY TO "GUILT" YOU INTO BUYING THEIR PRODUCT.

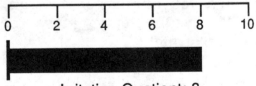

Irritation Quotient: 8

Sometimes an annoying phone solicitor will become even more annoying when he or she just won't take your negative hints.

24

You'll be talking to a guy who's trying to unload some American flags or designer garbage bags on you, and even though you've said "not interested" several times, he'll try to play on your emotions by saying something like, "Oh, but all the proceeds from these useful products are going to the Society for Anorexic Cats. Won't you please reconsider?"

Sometimes it gets tough, especially when the pitchperson represents a cause you're remotely interested in. But bothersome salespeople are bothersome salespeople, and despite the fact that your output of bucks *might* help Children Stuck in Puberty, the plain fact is, you don't want designer garbage bags, so the best solution is to order several dozen in the name of someone you don't like, then have them delivered to his home C.O.D.

PEOPLE WHO WON'T END A CONVERSATION WHEN THEY'RE THE ONES WHO CALLED *YOU*.

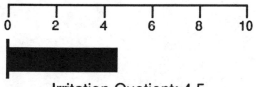

Irritation Quotient: 4.5

There is an unwritten rule in phone etiquette which states that the person initiating the phone call should be the one who officially ends it.

Unfortunately, loquacious individuals, motor-mouths and lonely people who don't have any other friends ignore this rule of common sense. Consequently, when a conversation begins to slow down or even grind to a silent halt, they'd rather just stay on the line until something else hits them than say, "Well, I better let you go."

SPs know when to end conversations because their sense of pacing and timing is usually keen. Waiting for someone else to end the chatter, though, can be infuriating, and the Superiors are usually the ones who have to finally say, "Look, I've gotta go. Call me back when you can't talk so long."

* * *

On top of all these telephonic problems, the final kick in the butt is the fact that this home irritation service isn't free of charge! You have to pay for it on an ongoing basis with your precious, hard-earned...

CATEGORY #4
MONEY
(It Makes the World Go Wrong)

Another tangible reality which affects Superior and Inferior alike is money. No one is above the power of those little pieces of paper and round metal tokens with pictures of old men on them. They dictate what every one of us does every day of the year, including leap year.

Everyone must acquire money somehow, some way, because if you don't, you can't buy clothes and food and insurance and deodorant and all those things needed for protection against the harsh world waiting just beyond your driveway.

Obviously, somebody somewhere took this need several steps further and publicly concluded, "Without money, an individual is worthless!" After all, that must be why some folks want it so desperately — so other people will think they're worth something.

It is this subconscious obsession with currency that causes several exasperating consequences. *Not having* money doesn't count. Naturally, being broke can be very annoying, but that can lead to things much too serious to be discussed in this book.

27

No, the following list is far less significant and far more maddening.

PAY DAYS THAT FALL ON MONDAY.

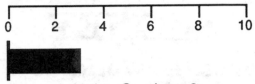

Irritation Quotient: 3

Some folks get a paycheck every week. Some folks get paid every two weeks, usually on Fridays. Those people don't know how fortunate they are.

Some get paid twice a month — on the 15th and the *last* day. SPs react negatively to this policy, usually when one of those pay days is on a Monday (i.e.: after the weekend has *ended,* when they would have had the most free time to go shopping, pay bills, etc.).

This irritation may sound a bit nit-picky, but remember, when you're a Superior Person, the slightest inconvenience has an effect on you ... just don't complain about this one *too* much. After all, you *are* still getting paid.

PEOPLE WHO WON'T COME RIGHT OUT AND ASK TO BORROW MONEY FROM YOU.

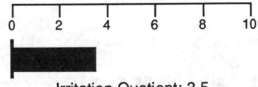

Irritation Quotient: 3.5

Perhaps people like this feel they are imposing when they ask to borrow five dollars for lunch. Their preliminary hemming and hawing may be a way of expressing guilt or shyness. What they don't realize is that same hemming and hawing along with all the blatant hints they're dropping are more of an emotional imposition than any material favor they could possibly request.

Just *ask*, dammit! Why wait for someone to ask *for* you??

But no, they'd rather adopt an expression conveying destitution and whine, "Boy, I wish I had enough to order that French Dip" or "Remember all those times I lent you bus fare?"

Tell 'em to just get it over with and stop all this provoking. Or else get a job.

PEOPLE WHO FORGET THEY BORROWED MONEY FROM YOU.

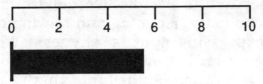

Irritation Quotient: 5.5

Ironically, it's those shy, self-conscious people who are the quickest to forget you loaned them money.

And you hate to remind someone of a loan you issued them, but when two or three weeks go by and they show no signs of monetary memory, you are then compelled to ask for your *own* money back so *you* can eat lunch — as if you needed a reason to want it back. Then the response is usually, "Oh yeah, I've been meaning to give it to you" or "Listen, uh, can I getcha back tomorrow?"

To which you and all Superior Moneylenders respond, "Sure," while looking for an opportunity to lift the billfold from his pocket or her purse, removing a credit card or two and going on a shopping binge.

GEE, YOU SHOULD'VE ASKED ME FOR THAT $50
BACK A COUPLE OF WEEKS AGO, BEFORE I
INVESTED IT ON "BLIND FAITH" IN THE FIFTH.

PEOPLE WHO HAVE DRAWN GRAFFITI OR DOODLED ON PAPER MONEY.

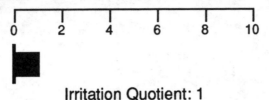

Irritation Quotient: 1

Not a big deal here, but it does make you wonder why people need to scrawl messages on currency, or blacken Alexander Hamilton's eye, or figure out their budget right on a bill, when there's plenty of scrap paper (and public restroom walls) in the world to use instead.

MAKING A PURCHASE AND RECEIVING CANADIAN COINS AS CHANGE.

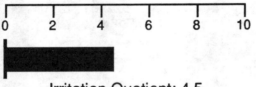

Irritation Quotient: 4.5

Vendors, businesses and regular people who slyly attempt to pass you Canadian coins when they give you change can be aggravating, especially if your mind is thinking about something else when they give it to you, and you don't notice what they've done until you get home.

Worry not. The easiest way to unload Canadian coins is to leave them as part of your tip in restaurants. Just make sure it's a place you're not planning to ever go back to.

DRIVING TEN MILES TO THE NEAREST "CONVENIENT" AUTOMATED TELLER ONLY TO FIND IT'S OUT OF ORDER.

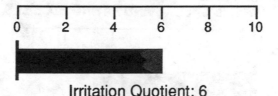

Irritation Quotient: 6

This is a terrible feeling, because you've come to this remote bank machine to get money for gas, which your car is now completely out of.

The usual self-defensive maneuver in this case is to hit or kick the machine and then impatiently look around to see if there's another one within walking distance. There isn't, needless to say, so you hurl yourself back into your car and gain a certain measure of revenge by driving as fast as you can on your way out of the deserted parking lot.

This irritation mutates into something stronger if you should find a machine that's out of *cash*, because here your reaction is delayed. You actually get to take your bank card out of your wallet or purse, insert it into the slot and go through the computerized rigmarole. Upon discovering the machine is fritzed, you contemplate shoving a slice of processed American cheese into the card slot to put it out of commission for good.

GETTING IN LINE AT THE BANK AUTO-TELLER BEHIND A PERSON WHO IS WITHDRAWING HIS LIFE'S SAVINGS, CASHING TWELVE CHECKS AND PAYING SIX BILLS.

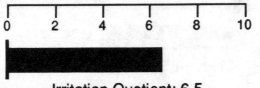

Irritation Quotient: 6.5

One of the most ignored signs in existence is the one in the auto-teller window which states: "Please limit your business to one or two transactions."

Granted, the auto-teller line is for lazy people, but not for lazy people who take an hour to do their banking. It can be quite bothersome to wait behind a slowpoke while breathing in his noxious exhaust fumes. The annoyance is compounded when you finally decide you've had enough and attempt to get out of line in order to park and walk inside. It is at that precise moment another vehicle will pull up behind you, sufficiently blocking you in.

BEING SEVENTEENTH IN LINE IN A BANK AND SEEING THAT NINE OF THE TEN WINDOWS HAVE "NEXT TELLER PLEASE" SIGNS IN FRONT OF THEM.

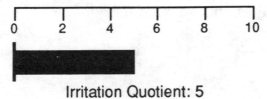

Irritation Quotient: 5

34

This situation occurs most often when you're in a hurry, and if you don't actually do this yourself, there's bound to be *somebody* in line who will turn to a total stranger and comment, "Why don't they hire more (bleeping) tellers?"

Silly question! If they did that, everyone would get along and life would be easier! As it is, there's only one teller open and you can count at least four employees at their desks ... *filing*. Of course, they don't see *you*. If they did, they'd jump to their feet and rush to open a few more windows, right?

Wrong ... so you'd better figure on being late for everything else you had planned that day.

* * *

Ultimately, it's up to you to decide which is more important: money-related irritations or poverty-related irritations. 999,999 SPs out of a million will usually opt for the former. And if you're one of those SPs, you will unfortunately require the following...

CATEGORY #5
WORK/JOB
(Losing the Rat Race)

Of all the categories covered in this book, this is the only one that irritates all by itself.

Unlike the necessity just studied —money— the job annoys and frustrates simply because it *exists*. All the other headaches that come *because* of the job are fringe (non)benefits.

You see, Superiors hate "working" for a living because it gets too regimented and routine too quickly. That's why a good number of them change jobs frequently in their never-ending quest to find that position which lets them get paid for doing things they really enjoy.

So, for the purpose of becoming the most Superior white- or blue-collar worker you can be, here are some prime work-related vexations for comparing and contrasting:

EXPLAINING TO PEOPLE WHY YOU'RE NOT DOING WHAT YOU MAJORED IN IN COLLEGE.

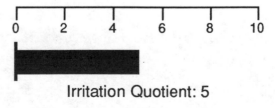

Irritation Quotient: 5

Forever telling people — especially relatives who have kept a close eye on your personal history — the reasons why you're not working at the trade / craft / career you were trained for can be frustrating, embarrassing and immensely tiresome.

People change their minds frequently throughout their lives, and Superiors often have uncommon talents which aren't always in demand *all* the time, so frequently they have to take what they can get while continually looking for that "Perfect Job."

But when closed-minded or ignorant acquaintances and kin keep yammering about why you haven't "made it" yet, or about how you "don't know what you want," it can be quite an angering state of affairs. You just want to slap them silly and yell, "I know what I'm doing!"

Even if you don't.

EMERGENCY MEETINGS CALLED TEN MINUTES BEFORE QUITTING TIME.

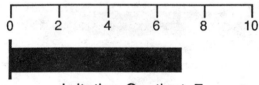

Irritation Quotient: 7

Home life? Dinner? Spare time????? What's that???

Sure, there are the clock-watchers: Those people who verbally count down the seconds to quitting time so they can be on the highway before anybody even knows they're gone. Then at the other end of the spectrum are the "My Job Is My Life" people, who don't know when to give it a rest, because:

1) They've got nothing else to do.

2) They're greedy.

3) They're just plain obsessed.

SPs are somewhere in the middle. In a sentence, Superiors value their free time.

So when last-minute meetings are called (which often turn out to be confabs that could have waited another 16 hours), Superior People can be seen contemplating just how easy it would be for one person to flip over the conference table exactly at 5 o'clock ... as a sign that the meeting is adjourned.

PEOPLE WHO WHISTLE OR HUM ALONG WITH OFFICE MUZAK.

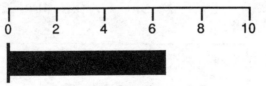

Irritation Quotient: 6.5

While humming and whistling are quite common in offices, the grating effect it has on the Superior Person is three times as intense if the "tunesmith" in question is accompanying an easy-listening station or Muzak tape.

For some reason, if the person is humming to an *original* song, the feeling isn't as bad.

This must be because Muzak in and of itself is annoying, especially to anyone who enjoys the original tunes from which the bastardized versions are derived. When someone hums to these one-dimensional songs, the Superior Person immediately assumes that the *offender* must be a one-dimensional *individual.*

And, more often than not, this entire grating effect is compounded because the person is humming off key.

PEOPLE WHO CAN'T FUNCTION UNLESS THEY GET THAT CUP OF COFFEE.

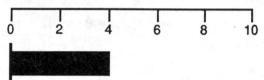

Irritation Quotient: 4

Superior People have no problem with coffee-drinkers. Many SPs drink coffee themselves. But Java Junkies? Coffee Achievers? Caffeine-heads? These individuals are very different.

One of the great overlooked addictions of the late 20th century directly affects what goes on at your workplace. It's also distracting to you when you see how the Quest for Coffee affects the behavior of some of your fellow employees.

Just watch the hallway when you first get into work tomorrow. Before too long you'll see someone trotting past. He's not going to the bathroom or to somebody's office for an important meeting — he's heading straight for the coffee machine so he can find the strength to face the day.

Seeing the glazed look on some coffee addict's face tells you it's appropriate that the majority of coffee beans come from Colombia.

PEOPLE WHO, ON MONDAYS, OFFER "IT'S MONDAY" AS AN EXCUSE FOR EVERYTHING THEY DO WRONG.

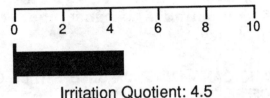

Irritation Quotient: 4.5

This one is annoying because it's so damned predictable.

Everyone who immediately spews, "Hey, whattaya want, it's Monday!" does so because they have been programmed to say it. These are the same Cliché People who get tired and careless at the end of the week and gripe, "Hey, whattaya want, it's Friday!" And on Wednesday when things go wrong, they spout, "Hey, whattaya want, it's Hump Day!"

Hey, hump *this.*

No matter what day of the week it may be, you *know* their bad performance is due to incompetence, clumsiness, or general inferiority.

PEOPLE WHO DON'T RELOAD THE COPY MACHINE AFTER THEY'VE USED ALL THE PAPER.

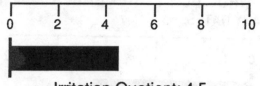

Irritation Quotient: 4.5

This is your basic irritation at someone else's laziness. It's also one that's widely experienced by the general working public, making it acceptable to visibly display. Getting uptight in this instance guarantees you'll get no strange looks or comments from co-workers, and you might even receive a little sympathy.

Regardless, this discourteous act makes you want to collate the offender's body parts.

PROFESSIONAL RECEPTIONISTS WHO ARE ANYTHING BUT PROFESSIONAL.

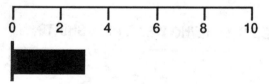

Irritation Quotient: 3

It's always curious to discover a business that hires a receptionist who is rude or short with customers and clients.

A good receptionist is vitally important to a company. She is often the first person people meet when contacting the office. To be hassled or snubbed by some snooty-do nail-filer can be quite grating. One doesn't need to wonder what talents she used to get the job in the first place.

BOSSES WHO DON'T REMEMBER EMPLOYMENT ANNIVERSARY DATES.

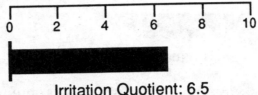

Irritation Quotient: 6.5

Some bosses will remember every detail about what you did wrong today, and will not hesitate to jump on you when they don't agree with your work methods.

But get 'em to give you an annual or semi-annual raise on time, and you will have pulled off one of the major business coups of the year.

Not all bosses are like this, of course, but isn't it funny how the ones that are end up being *your* bosses?

MALE EXECUTIVES WHO WEAR PINK SHIRTS.

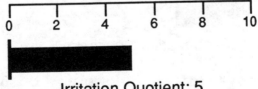

Irritation Quotient: 5

Here's an annoyance you *cannot* blatantly display in the workplace, especially if you're a subordinate. There's nothing inherently wrong with the color pink, but there *is* something terribly vexing about trendy executives who wear pink dress shirts.

Most of these mannequin-like "suits" are totally caught up in playing the *part* of an executive (i.e. they use buzzwords like "let's do lunch," "I'll take a meeting" and "is that S.O.P.?" — a cool-sounding abbreviation for Standard Operating Procedure). Performing job functions is of secondary importance to these "players." They're also the ones who can tell you what the term "Fortune-500" actually means.

All this hooey makes them sound arrogant and phony. Add to the fact that most of these plastic people wear pink designer shirts, and the result is a set of prime targets for your spite. After awhile, you automatically associate pink shirts with pretentiousness, so when you spot a three-piece stranger with a pink shirt walking down the hall, you already resent him even *before* he orders you to get him a cup of coffee.

PEOPLE WHO HAVE RISEN TO EXECUTIVE POWER DESPITE HAVING LITTLE OR NO TALENT OR INTELLIGENCE.

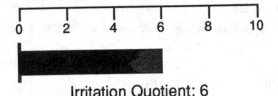

Irritation Quotient: 6

This irritation goes one step further than the Pink Shirt Phenomenon because, even though an executive might wear a disgusting pink shirt, he still may be deserving of his executive position. It's that male or female who is incompetent as an executive that makes this emotional distress even more consuming.

These "pretend important people" with zero managerial skills clearly dispel their credibility every time they open their mouths. But they make life miserable for all *true* Superior People. They force you to do pointless tasks, shamelessly draw attention to all the pretentious accouterments which decorate their office, speak in high and mighty exec jargon and, amazingly, actually believe that under all the blah-blah harumphing, they're good at what they do and deserve to be treated differently than everyone else.

One small consolation to the Superior Subordinate is that it's usually very plain to all present that this "imitation bigwig" is an unqualified idiot. Because of that — and the old adage that there is safety in numbers — this person is eventually gang-ignored, and will disappear after his first major screw-up.

44

BROWN-NOSERS.

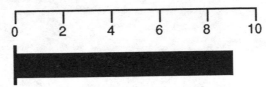

Irritation Quotient: 9

In the business world, the only color worse than pink is brown, particularly when it's located on the end of an employee's proboscis.

There is probably nothing more enraging to a true SP than a weasel who blatantly sucks up to the boss and tries to put him or herself ahead of everyone else on his level. When the brown-noser resorts to snitching on people to try to get ahead, what they really deserve is getting their brown schnozz turned to a bright, throbbing shade of red.

* * *

Speaking of work, experts tell you never to go to bed with anybody at the office. (Go to a motel, for God's sake!) Seriously, that practice can only lead to trouble, or at the very least, discomfort.

But the office isn't the only place where human biology can lead to problems. For Superior Persons, sex can cause considerable anguish, and they don't even have to be one of the consenting adults...

CATEGORY #6:
SEX
(... Sex? Sex!)

It was only a matter of time before this category rolled around. Yes, it's true, one of life's most pleasurable experiences can be irritating (other than by infections and rashes).

Before probing this list of irritants, some guidelines must be laid down. Obviously, many facets of physical love and humans being sexually active can be exacerbating — like forgetting to take your pill or neglecting to don your condom — in the long run, those can be *real* annoying. This chapter, however, will not concentrate on the graphic, Tab-A-into-Slot-B side of sex. What *will* be discussed are the more openly social examples of people as sexual beings: Specifically, folks who try to pass themselves off as something they're not.

Most individuals want to be known as people who like sex. Superior People surely do, proven by the fact that they approach sexual topics with subtle humor, cleverness and class.

Inferior People either aren't sure if they like sex or are insecure about their sexuality so, in an effort to mask their anxieties (and exhibit a false front), make sexual topics extremely dominant in any conversation that might crop

47

up. What's more, they treat these topics with crassness, loudness and blatant disregard for other people's feelings. Sure, everyone makes jokes about sex, but the Inferior Crude Attitude is based on chauvinistic opinions and misconceptions.

That spelled out, here are the primary irritations regarding sex — or, more to the point — people who promote false sex:

FEMALES WHO WANT TO HAVE SEX WITH HEAVY METAL MUSICIANS.

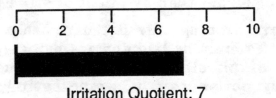

Irritation Quotient: 7

This one confuses most males who are to some degree concerned with hygiene. Why would a girl (usually aged 15 to 19) want to defile herself with a gross slime-bucket in tight leather pants who only knows four chords?

You will often notice this desire in females becomes very vocal when a few girlfriends are around. With a sympathetic audience present, a teen-age girl isn't nearly as embarrassed to stand in a record store for hours and burn holes in the latest heavy metal band poster with her mascara-caked eyes.

MEN WHO MUST CONSTANTLY CONVINCE MALE FRIENDS OF THEIR MASCULINITY BY BLATANTLY DROOLING OVER ANY REMOTELY-ATTRACTIVE WOMAN ON THE STREET.

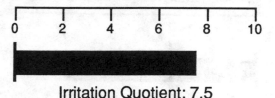

Irritation Quotient: 7.5

This is quite a bother, not only to women but to any self-respecting male with gonadal control.

Picture this all-too-common scenario: You're a man riding in a car with two male co-workers on the way to a crucial meeting. You're discussing the upcoming presentation when suddenly the talking abruptly halts, all heads turn to the left (including yours, being a man), and one of the guys says, "Oh yeaaaaahhh, walk a little slower, baby," to which the other one responds, "Man, I'd like to poke her tonight," upon which your neck muscles tighten, your teeth clench and your sarcastic mind says, "Why wait until tonight?? Why not go over and jump on her right now, big guy?!"

Now keep in mind, whether a male is Superior or not, he's still a *male*. If a man sees a woman and thinks to *himself* how pretty she is, what a nice body she has and how well she'd probably perform in bed, that's okay. That's just how the normal male animal thinks. The difference is, the Superior Man doesn't need to rudely *vocalize* it to prove his manhood.

49

MEN WHO MAKE SEXUAL COMMENTS TOWARD WOMEN WALKING DOWN THE STREET, BUT WHO WOULD CURL UP AND DIE IF ONE OF THEM RESPONDED TO THEIR ADVANCES.

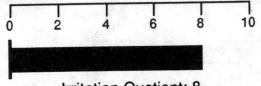

Irritation Quotient: 8

Here's a situation that goes one step further — and one notch more infuriating — than the last item.

Just once it would be satisfying to see a guy make a lecherous comment directly to a woman and then have her turn, push him to the ground and say, "You got it, pal! Let's go! Right here, right now!" You would then enjoy witnessing the ex-stud melt from the complex human-shape he was using as a disguise into simple liquid slime. He would not have the slightest clue how to handle it.

Then you could applaud the obviously "together" woman and take her out to lunch.

OKAY — YOU'RE ON, PAL! RIGHT HERE, RIGHT NOW!
C'MON, LET'S GO!

MEN WHO THINK "FOREPLAY" IS ASKING A WOMAN OUT FOR A DATE.

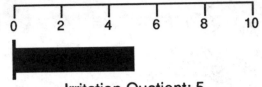

Irritation Quotient: 5

MEN WHO THINK "ROMANCE" IS WHAT GOES ON IN PORNO MOVIES.

Irritation Quotient: 5.5

Both of these items emphasize the stereotype that in a relationship, women want romance and men want climaxes.

Unfortunately for women, stereotypes are often true. Unfortunately for SPs of *both* sexes, men who openly behave like that's the way it should be can be found on every corner. Their embarrassing philosophy makes you want to find a jar of pepperoncinis and dump it down their pants.

WOMEN WHO ACT DISGUSTED WHEN CO-WORKERS MAKE OFF-COLOR JOKES, BUT WHO GO TO MALE STRIP JOINTS THREE NIGHTS A WEEK.

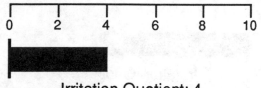

Irritation Quotient: 4

This annoyance is of the head-shaking variety. A woman who subscribes to this brand of prudish hypocrisy also attends the "I-can't-have-it-so-I'll-publicly-fantasize-about-it" school of social behavior.

The pang of intolerance is felt when she tries to make everyone think she's an innocent virgin when someone tells a dirty joke. Why does she do this? Is there a subconscious need to live up to some 1940s pure-as-snow attitude? Does she believe people will think she's less than a "lady" if she laughs? Obviously not, since somehow everyone knows she slips ten-spots into burly dancers' G-strings every Monday, Wednesday and Friday night.

MEN WHO, IN ALL SERIOUSNESS, USE WORDS LIKE "FOX," "BABE" AND "PIECE."

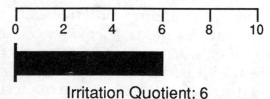

Irritation Quotient: 6

WOMEN WHO, IN ALL SERIOUSNESS, USE WORDS LIKE "HUNK," "BEEFCAKE" AND "STUD."

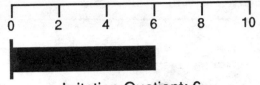

Irritation Quotient: 6

Impersonal sexual monikers such as these are perturbing when utilized by men who actually believe the definition of "Fox," "Babe" and "Piece" is woman.

However, as slang synonyms, they grow increasingly humorous the more you picture what the words actually *do* mean. It's doubtful any man would want to be found in bed with the personification of *any* of those three words — especially "piece," which could end up being almost anything you'd see in a *Friday the 13th* flick.

As far as women are concerned, fave nicknames for the dudes are "Hunk," "Beefcake" and "Stud."

Now, everyone knows what necrophilia is, but what do you call making love to raw meat? Or horses? Only women who use these male synonyms know for sure.

Yes, the name-calling practice can work for women as well as men, as evidenced by these three popular words. Hearing them can also accelerate the Superior Person's heart, pulse and breathing rate. No, that's not a description of sexual excitement. It's pure irritation.

PREHISTORIC BEHAVIOR AT BACHELOR/BACHELORETTE PARTIES.

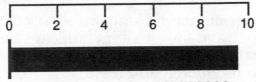

Irritation Quotient: 9.999999

The sexual posturings that go on at these things are the main reason for this item's inclusion in this category, but there is much more to get irate about than that.

The Bachelor Party: A group of males — some strangers, some friends — commune for an evening of voyeurism and mock sexual excitement, all to pay "last respects" to a mutual chum who, horror of horrors, is getting married!

On the distaff side, more and more women these days are throwing "Bachelorette Parties" for the bride-to-be so they can say they all had a bit of guilty fun, too. Those shindigs feature male strippers, kinky gag gifts and a cake shaped like a penis but, try as they might, they cannot compare to the long, jaded history of the Male Bachelor Party and what goes on there. Don't be surprised when one day scientists discover that every insidious sexually-transmitted disease known to the world came into existence at a bachelor party.

Many Superior Males hate bachelor parties for a number of reasons:

1) They have a difficult time feigning Cro-Magnon-like machismo and feeling good about it.

2) They do not get uncontrollably drunk, and so have no way of hiding behind an artificial substance to make the occasion even remotely interesting.

3) They have quality sex on a regular basis and have a minimal desire to ogle a third-rate stripper.

4) They find the prospect of watching hard-core porno flicks with a roomful of *men* decidedly unappealing.

5) They simply find these mandatory bashes as boring as hell.

Unfortunately, there is one big reason why an SP *will* go to a bachelor party: He was invited, and doesn't want to hurt the groom's (his friend's) feelings by not showing up.

Regardless of why or how long you are there, however, it can be said that, for you, the Superior Person, there is indeed one universally positive occurrence at each and every bachelor/bachelorette party: The Moment You Leave.

* * *

Another more practical problem in the world of sex is that much of it is of the promiscuous variety. And as fate would have it, promiscuous sex goes with our next category like drugs and ... our next category. Or like dishonesty and...

CATEGORY #7:

SHOW BUSINESS

(Like No Business
We Care to Know)

Show bizz is chock full of especially irritating people, who then influence *everyday* people to become irritating as well. The recording industry, movies and TV and everything they touch can at once be highly entertaining and powerfully infuriating.

We'll now peruse the most maddening aspects of today's popular electronic culture for the Superior Person of the 1990s and beyond.

PEOPLE WHO LIKE ROCK MUSICIANS FOR THEIR BRASH-NESS OR CLOTHES FIRST, AND FOR THEIR MUSIC *LAST*.

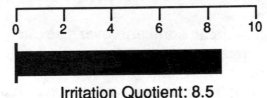

Irritation Quotient: 8.5

Musicianship is often last on the list of reasons why people like rock musicians. Many teenage boys like hard rock not because the music is necessarily good or because its attitudes speak for them; they like it because it's **loud**. They want to

57

get back at Mom and Dad for the crime of being parents, so volume is of major importance when selecting a group to pledge devotion to. This is annoying behavior, but some consolation can be gained from the fact that someday, *their* kids will be confronting them with a new, more outrageous form of noise (if they don't overdose first, of course.)

Inferior teenage girls, on the other hand, base their affection for a musician on the cling factor of his jeans and the length of his teased hair. And they'll buy all the tunes and go to all the concerts — not because the band plays tight, but because the lead singer's *butt* is tight.

PEOPLE WHO LIKE A PARTICULAR POPULAR SONG BECAUSE THEY "CAN DANCE TO IT."

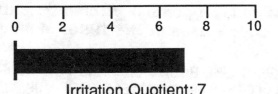

Irritation Quotient: 7

When you hear someone over the age of 10 say they like a particular song "because it's got a good beat" or because "I can dance to it," and you are convinced their comment was sincere, it's time to get angry, launch into a loud harangue and begin bending their records and CDs to the breaking point until that person completely reforms.

Due to the resurrection of Disco, repackaged and hyped as "Dance Music" and "Club Music," the mentality of the average record buyer has descended to the level of the dance floor. Airheads everywhere have reunited en masse to inform you that the beat is all you need to have a satisfying musical experience.

Never mind about melodies. Forget about tunes with thought-provoking or socially-significant lyrics. Just thump that bass, baby!

Don't misunderstand — there's nothing wrong with a song you can dance to. But if that's all a song has to offer, it's like eating a rotten malted milk ball: It looks nice on the outside, but the second you sink your teeth into it, it leaves a bad taste in your mouth.

PEOPLE WHO DEIFY RECORDING ARTISTS.

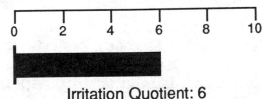

Irritation Quotient: 6

In 1966 when John Lennon said the Beatles were more popular than Jesus Christ, the establishment was outraged at what appeared to be a blatantly sacrilegious statement.

Ironically, today that statement can be applied to dozens of musical acts, but no one bats an eye. Between Jon Bon Jovi, Michael Jackson, Prince, Madonna, Whitney Houston, Debbie Gibson, Run-DMC, This Week's Heavy Metal Superstar, etcetera, etcetera, millions of young boys and girls practically devote their lives to the poster shrines they've erected in their rooms.

This same irritation blindly emanates from the lost souls who go to Graceland every year to kiss Elvis' tombstone, or those who think the King is very much alive, pumping gas somewhere in northern Wisconsin.

One day it will be time for all these people to get lives, and then where will they be? Probably bothering *you* with some new obsession.

THE ATTACK OF THE DRUM MACHINES.

```
0    2    4    6    8    10
```

Irritation Quotient: 9.5

The drum machine almost single-handedly ripped the guts out of rock music in the 1980s. The imitation percussive effect of this contraption is cold, impersonal, anything but spontaneous, and it deprives real flesh-and-blood drummers of work.

Drum machines and the recent overuse of synthesizers in recorded music are tearing down what rock and roll was supposed to be in the first place: exciting. And you can thank all those folks who like songs they "can dance to" for the onslaught of electric keyboard-based robot music which now plagues radio waves and record stores.

What's next? Synthesized songwriters?

MUSIC CRITICS WHO GET SONG TITLES AND NAMES OF ARTISTS WRONG.

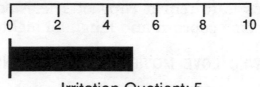

Irritation Quotient: 5

Music reviewers are supposed to be credible sources of criticism, purporting to give insightful and well-researched views about musicians' work — both positive and negative. However, when you read a review containing wrong song titles or a band member ignorantly misidentified, you can always achieve a modicum of satisfaction by crumbling the "Entertainment" pages of the newspaper and moving on to the sports section.

FILM CRITICS WHO RAVE ABOUT SUBTITLED FOREIGN FILMS THAT ARE THREE-AND-A-HALF HOURS LONG.

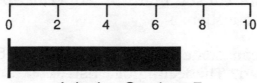

Irritation Quotient: 7

Superiors usually have some degree of culture in them, but come on.

This is a major *botheration*, and hearing Gene and Roger go on and on about the latest Norwegian film which tells the tender story of a love triangle in a Scandinavian mining town during the 1920s makes you want to switch channels real quick. Who can relate to this kind of stuff? (Besides old, love-starved Scandinavians, that is.)

When this happens, a sure cure for the foreign film blues is to rent a copy of *The Naked Gun*, explode some popcorn and laugh all night.

PEOPLE WHO LOVE MOVIES WHICH ARE INCREDIBLY AWFUL.

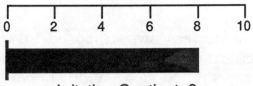

Irritation Quotient: 8

(Not hilariously awful movies — just *awful* awful ones.)

See, Superior People have excellent taste. Be it wine, food, people, music, films or anything else, Superiors know what they like and it's always redeeming or worthwhile in some respect. This good taste causes many a Superior to ask the following question:

How can some people be so blind? So unsophisticated? The feeling of frustration and futility which sweeps through your very being when someone says they loved a movie you found appallingly bad is a very unique sensation.

For instance: When somebody tells you they thought the sequels to *Poltergeist* were better than the original movie. Or someone saying that *Mannequin* was pretty damn funny.

It works the other way, too: In a discussion about classic American films, watch out for the clown who announces that he or she thought *Citizen Kane* was "boring."

You're never going to change their short-sighted opinion in cases like these, so just be irritated and change the subject to something emotionally harmless, like politics.

STAND-UP COMEDIANS WHO LAUGH AT THEIR OWN JOKES.

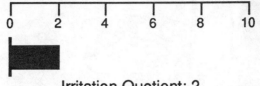

Irritation Quotient: 2

It is important to recognize that while watching a stand-up comedy routine in person or on the tube, it can be very distracting to hear the comedian guffaw at something he or she just said. It usually means they're full of themselves or they don't think their material is very strong. To be fair, they're usually both true.

...SO THEN SHE SAID — ARE YOU READY FOR THIS?
— "OH, YEAH? WELL THEN WHO'S THAT IN THE
CAKE?" HOO! HAH! IS THAT FUNNY, OR WHAT?!

PEOPLE WHO EARN MONEY BEING A CELEBRITY LOOK-ALIKE.

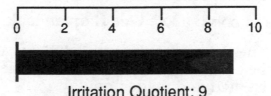

Irritation Quotient: 9

This is one of the most galling, insane-making phenomena to become a reality in the last decade for the following reasons:

1) Unlike most other irritations, it isn't natural, accidental or coincidental. This act is totally premeditated. People who leech off other people's success must carefully plan out their course of action.

2) It points out the lengths (or depths) third-rate would-be actors will go to be in show business. They refuse to be in another line of work and are not talented enough to be original, so they pretend to be an already existing famous person.

PEOPLE WHO MAKE A LIVING IMITATING SOMEONE ELSE'S ORIGINAL *CHARACTER*.

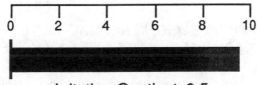

Irritation Quotient: 9.5

This dubious career choice is even worse than being a celebrity look-alike because it's one rung lower on the Leech Ladder.

Case in point: a Pee Wee Herman look-alike...

1) The imitator isn't even doing a real person; he's ripping off a character someone *else* created and made popular.

2) It's always a bad third-generation imitation.

3) He's getting paid for this bastardization.

Very often, this annoyance first manifests itself in childhood, when you go to a grand opening of a new McDonald's restaurant and realize the guy in the clown suit passing out balloons is not the *real* Ronald McDonald from TV. This one has a low, gruff voice, yells at the kids and smokes a cigar. With this deeply entrenched in your memory, as an adult you can't resist detesting other character plagiarizers.

This is why, on Halloween, you'll never catch SPs dressing up as a character like Batman or Freddy Krueger or anybody else with a "™" beside their name. It's got to be an original costume ... or buck nakedness.

ORDINARY PEOPLE WHO, IN NORMAL CONVERSATION, USE TO EXCESS POPULAR TV AND MOVIE CATCH-PHRASES.

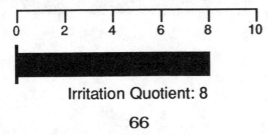

Irritation Quotient: 8

It's a sure bet that even the good-natured Billy Crystal has gotten bent out of shape at this one. This type of vexation occurs when any popular character's catch-phrase is overused (usually in an exaggerated delivery) by an everyday person in conversation — especially when repeated to excess. Like the comedian who laughs at his own jokes, this habit belies a lack of originality, only here it's in everyday communication.

Mimicked lines which are certain to produce an irking effect in your hometown are:

Crystal's "You look mahvelous."

John Lovitz's "Yeah, that's it, that's the ticket."

Dana Carvey's "Isn't that special?"

Carvey's and Kevin Nealon's "We want to pump (clap) *you* up!"

Clint Eastwood's "Make my day."

Steve Martin's "Excuuuuuuuuuuse me!" (Yes, even today.)

The butchering of these examples offers proof that signature phrases should be allowed to be copyrighted by their creators. While it has been said that "imitation is the greatest form of flattery," the world would be better off with a few less of these *monkeys*.

MUSIC VIDEOS WHICH PURPORT TO BE "LIVE PERFORM-ANCES," BUT WHICH ARE OBVIOUSLY LIP-SYNCHED.

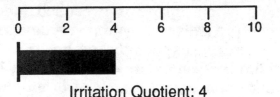

Irritation Quotient: 4

Music videos as an "art form" can often be irritating, what with everybody and his heavy metal brother wanting to get into the act — to say nothing of the fact that the visual "story" or images often have absolutely nothing to do with the song.

But nothing in music videos plays more on the gullibility of the audience than the clips that try to make you believe the song you're hearing is a live concert performance.

Metal bands almost always present their videos this way: They shoot the clip in an auditorium on stage in front of thousands of people, yet it's obvious the group is lip-synching to the original recorded version of the song. Since the crew and extras went to all the trouble of setting up in a hall, why don't they just hook up the microphones and record them playing live?

Answer? Because live, the band basically blows.

ANTI-DRUG PUBLIC SERVICE ANNOUNCEMENTS PRESENTED BY ROCK MUSICIANS.

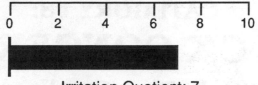

Irritation Quotient: 7

It's now chic to be somebody who's been a substance abuser since birth, allegedly kick the habit and go on TV to proudly announce you've realized coke and grass are bad for your health. To be fair, in some cases this is undoubtedly a true story.

But to see a half-brain-dead rocker who has the permanent sniffles telling you and your kids drugs aren't cool ... somehow that just doesn't ring true.

Rockers Against Drugs ... undoubtedly an organization that's listed in Guinness as having the world's smallest membership.

* * *

There's an old showbiz adage: "Give the people what they want." Well, this is probably a big reason there's so much that's annoying about the entertainment industry ... the audience _itself_ *is annoying.*

And man, there's no better place to prove that theory than in the rock and roll arena. You don't even need a ticket...

CATEGORY #8:
ROCK CONCERTS
(Ooh, That Smell ...)

The next eight categories of everyday irritations focus primarily on different types of social interaction. Each of the eight involves coming in contact with large numbers of people at any given time. And you know what happens when groups of Superior and Inferior Folks interact...

The first of these social examples is the Rock Concert. While some of the items listed here can apply to classical music performances, sports events and plays, it is rock concerts which elicit every one of these irritations, mainly because rock concerts attract the most inferior, undesirable low-lifes imaginable.

It's sad to conclude that the majority of people who go to rock concerts aren't there for the reason Superior People are: to hear good music.

PEOPLE WHO LIGHT UP A JOINT THE MOMENT THE HOUSE LIGHTS DIM.

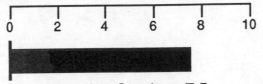

Irritation Quotient: 7.5

To a majority of conditioned inferior rock concertgoers, lights going out in the hall means not only that the show is about to start but that it's also time to ignite the Beloved Roach. Some of these individuals light up so fast, you'd think they were afraid to hear one chord of music without being under some sort of chemical influence. Within seconds, that sweet, intrusive odor comes wafting your way, and by the end of the show you've got a vicarious buzz, along with a headache and a case of cotton mouth.

Once outside, it's great to inhale actual air again. At this point, look around and you'll see many puzzled burnouts trying to figure out what that new smell is.

It's called "oxygen."

PEOPLE WHO PAY FIFTY DOLLARS TO SEE A CONCERT, THEN ARRIVE A HALF-HOUR OR MORE LATE.

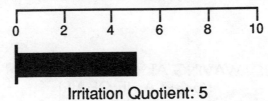

Irritation Quotient: 5

71

I'M *NOT* WAVING AT YOU — I'M JUST TRYING
TO GET A HIT OF AIR!

Concerts are unique events. They involve a live performer whom you as a spectator will never witness the same way again. Why then, are there so many people who show up late for a special event like this?

These are not the ones who are making their way to their seats when the first song starts, or even the visibly upset individuals who look as though they were unavoidably detained in traffic. Those in question are the blank-faced dweebs who waltz in 30 to 45 minutes after the show starts and act as though they haven't missed anything!

Why are they even here? Why did they spend the money? Don't they care about the musician(s) they laid out big money to see (or not see, depending on your seat)? Why didn't they leave home extra early? Why didn't they just *stay* home? If not for them, we might have had better seats!

PEOPLE WHO WERE TOO CHEAP TO BUY THEIR OWN PROGRAM, SO ASK TO LOOK AT YOURS.

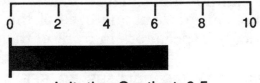

Irritation Quotient: 6.5

"Hey man, can I see your program?" (Notice, they never say *read*. It's always "see.")

The first few times this happens to you, you're usually unprepared for the imposition and, as a genuinely kind person, you have no real choice but to hand it over. The *last* time it happens, it's because you discover the borrower is using the ten-dollar collector's item as camouflage while he rolls a joint.

Just pretend you're reading it right up until showtime so no cheapskate moron bugs you for it. Better yet, be smart, buy it *after* the concert.

PEOPLE WHO TAKE FLASH PICTURES FROM THE BACK OF THE HALL.

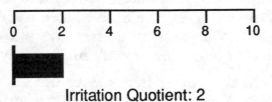

Irritation Quotient: 2

These geniuses are the same people who take pictures of Niagara Falls at night with their instamatic flash cameras.

Don't you wish you could see the look on their faces when they eagerly pick up their concert prints at Fotomat, only to find that instead of beautiful candid shots of the band, they've got washed-out, out-of-focus pictures of the backs of the heads of the spectators in front of them?

PEOPLE WHO PAY BIG DOLLARS TO SEE A FAMOUS MUSICIAN, THEN GET UP TO BUY A BEER DURING EVERY SONG THEY DON'T RECOGNIZE.

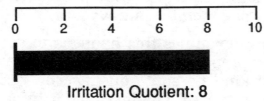

Irritation Quotient: 8

This is both maddening and confusing. Super-iors go to a concert because they appreciate the artist's music. They're apparently in the minority because without fail, the second a song starts that isn't a "hit" or a "classic," dozens of people stand up and head for the concession stands!

Terms like "showmanship" and "artistic state-ment" are lost on these superficial jerks. These are people who only care about hit singles: The ones who attend an Elton John concert *only* to hear "Your Song"; the ones who go to a Pink Floyd show *only* to hear "Money." The rest of the time is spent sucking down the brew.

An effective deterrent for all such offenders would be to equip the seats with belts or harness bars like those on roller coasters, which would comfortably but securely keep antsy-pantsy audience members where they should be until show's end — in a seated position.

PEOPLE IN YOUR ROW WHO, DURING THE SHOW, GET UP AND DECIDE TO WALK IN FRONT OF *YOU*.

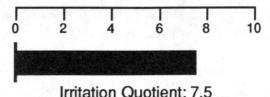

Irritation Quotient: 7.5

Someone exiting a row while the show is in progress is annoying enough, but it's even more irritating when that person is in *your* row and decides to leave via the space containing *your* seat.

75

By choosing to exit through your territory, they're also blocking your vision, and they usually get stuck for a few seconds directly in front of you, affording you a primo view of their crotch or buttocks.

Just remember to bring a pin with you next time.

BURNOUTS AND OBNOXIOUS TEENAGERS WHO SCREAM "YEEEEAAAAAAH!" EVERY TIME THE WORDS "SEX" OR "DRUGS" ARE SUNG.

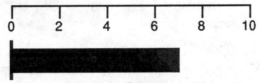

Irritation Quotient: 7

In an effort to stand out from the crowd, this class of sub-human likes to draw attention to itself by verbally expressing its approval at every sexually-oriented and narcotic-related reference the singer utters.

What these dullards don't realize is they're standing out the same way a wart stands out.

PEOPLE DIRECTLY BETWEEN YOU AND THE STAGE WHO, FOR NO REASON, GIVE THEIR OWN PERSONAL STANDING OVATION EVERY FEW MINUTES.

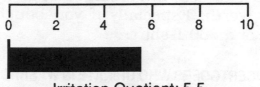

Irritation Quotient: 5.5

Individuals who stand up without provocation merely to raise their arms or clap or wave a cigarette lighter should be force-fed the butane in those lighters.

They never display any courtesy for the people around them but, then again, since this is a rock concert none should be expected. With any luck at all, these bozos will just pass out quietly.

PROFESSIONAL ACTS THAT PLAY LESS THAN NINETY MINUTES.

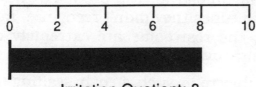

Irritation Quotient: 8

For the greenbacks you shell out to see a rock show these days, you deserve not only a quality performance, but one of reasonable quantity as well.

Two hours should be the mandatory length for a band to play, but anything less than 90 minutes should be treated with loud boos and hisses from the audience. Nothing violent, mind you, just strong vocal disapproval.

It's one way to blow off steam accumulated from this irritation, but it still won't give you your money's worth. Especially if you bought a $25 program or a $60 T-shirt.

MALE CONCERTGOERS WHO URINATE IN WASHROOM SINKS.

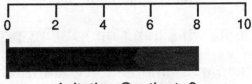

Irritation Quotient: 8

A habit as incredibly fascinating as it is uniquely exclusive to rock concerts is the act of urinating in a receptacle other than a urinal.

Women, because of their biological construction, have limited options when it comes to post-concert bathroom behavior. But after a show, the guys hafta unload all the brewskis they inhaled during the tunes they didn't recognize, man. After concerts, the restrooms are extremely crowded, and certain guys gotta relieve themselves *now!*

Since they're in such a rush, waiting in line for a stall is out of the question, so they just unzip, stand on their toes and aim for the sink!

If you've never experienced this bizarre sight, it'll be an extra treat if you're initiated by witnessing a man who is a veteran sink pee-er. You'll marvel as he hits the target right from the first drop and, needless to say, he won't wash his hands when he's finished.

Now, if you're a veteran practical joker, think how much fun it would be to reach around him and turn on the water full blast. You then make a quick exit — but not too quick. If he's "midstream" he won't be able to chase after you.

TAKING NINETY SECONDS TO FIND A PARKING SPACE BEFORE THE SHOW, BUT TAKING NINETY *MINUTES* TO REACH THE EXIT *AFTER* THE SHOW.

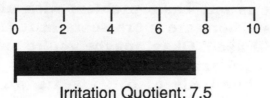

Irritation Quotient: 7.5

It has always been intriguing to note how smoothly cars file *into* an arena parking lot, but how you better have a full tank of gas and non-perishable food rations while you wait to get *out.*

That's why it's always better if someone else drives to the concert, so you can just go to sleep while he or she grips the steering wheel with bone-crushing pressure and curses at all the stoned half-wits trying to create their own exit. Smart SPs bring along a good book (like "War and Peace"). You'll probably finish it before you get out.

* * *

Concerts cost a lot of money and usually end up being more hassle-ridden than they're worth. Go see a movie instead. It's cheaper and you won't get as irritated.

Well, it's <u>cheaper</u>, anyway...

79

CATEGORY #9:
MOVIE THEATERS
(35-Millimeter Miseries)

There is one basic problem with all movie theaters: There are more seats in it than you alone will need. Okay, maybe you're bringing a date or your family. That still leaves dozens, possibly hundreds of other seats which you won't require, but which unfortunately *will* be filled with those other (inferior) moviegoers.

There are a few irritations which movie theaters have in common with concert halls. Those reliable folks who stand up and walk in front of you during the show are present, as well as the late-comers and early-goers. Still, the movie theater, because of the type of entertainment it offers, possesses several annoyances all its own.

TEENAGERS WHO ARRIVE TO SEE THE MOVIE WITH 27 OF THEIR CLOSEST FRIENDS.

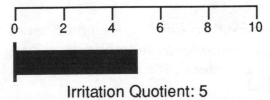

Irritation Quotient: 5

First of all, it's beyond comprehension that one kid can have *that* many friends. Second of all, they can't all be interested in the same film. Therefore, they must be in the theater for the sole purpose of bothering everybody else.

This gang of pubescent patrons usually sits near the front in one or perhaps two rows. These kids love to throw things at each other and at the screen — and traditionally make loud comments about the actors or action in the flick.

These individuals beg for somebody's wrath, especially from SPs who regard cinema as something of an art form.

How's this for a fantasy cure-all: While the teens go en masse to the restroom or concession stand, an usher puts Super Glue on each of their seats. The disruptive teens soon return and suddenly find themselves literally "riveted to their seats." Then, the rest of the civilized audience files out to the next theater as the opening credits begin for a six-hour foreign documentary.

THEATERS THAT ALLOW "UNATTENDED" ADOLESCENTS INTO R-RATED MOVIES.

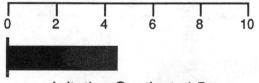

Irritation Quotient: 4.5

There are reasons for rules. The Film Ratings Board initiated the use of G, PG, PG-13, R and X for a specific purpose. Kids should be shielded from the violence and sex in a movie theater. Let 'em learn that stuff at home where it belongs.

An R-rated film means "restricted": Children under 17 are not to be admitted into the theater without parent or adult guardian. However, when attending an R-rated movie, you will invariably see that gang of 15-year-old kids or a group of ten year olds running up and down and across the aisles.

Superior Individuals' blood pressure rises when theaters let these kids into adult-oriented films. Never mind the effect the language, sex and violence has on *them* — they're bothering people when they shouldn't be there at all! You as a moviegoer have a right to your freedom from Children Under Seventeen! The R-rated movie (on paper, anyway) grants you that right, but you're denied it every time a child rushes by, screaming for caramel corn!

It's at those times that Superiors feel like throwing some R-rated language in the little terror's direction!

PARENTS WHO BRING SCREAMING INFANTS TO MOVIE THEATERS.

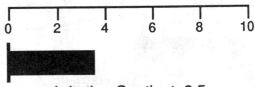

Irritation Quotient: 3.5

Wonderfully courteous moms and dads like these either couldn't get a babysitter or didn't want to pay one to watch their three-week-old kid, so the obvious alternative is to bring him to the theater!

So what if he screams over most of the dialogue? So what if they change his diaper right there in the twelfth row? Nobody'll mind ... 'cuz it's such a cute wittle baby!

After an hour and a half of this distraction, it's enough to cause you to fantasize about having a detonator ... and creating your own sequel to "Baby Boom."

PEOPLE WHO ARRIVE AT A CROWDED THEATER 30 MINUTES LATE, THEN ASK PERSONS IN EVERY ROW, "ARE THOSE SEATS TAKEN?"

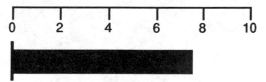

Irritation Quotient: 7.5

Here are those perpetually tardy folks again, but now they're even more irritating because, unlike at a concert, they don't have assigned seats — so they spend ten minutes looking around for a place to park their family. And since it's dark, they must stick their bulbous heads down every row and interrupt someone's concentration to ask if "those seats are taken."

By the time ample seating is found, all the family members have split up to start their own search, and must now be flagged down by means of arm-waving and loud whispering.

SAY, IS YOUR SEAT TAKEN?

At this point, all the SPs in the audience get very angry, causing one or two of them to call out in a stern voice, "Sit your (expletive) down!" Turning a deaf ear, the trouble-makers just go on about their annoying business, happy as clams.

Meanwhile, because of this distraction, you have missed an important plot development scene and spend the rest of the movie trying to figure out what exactly is going on.

STICKY THEATER FLOORS.

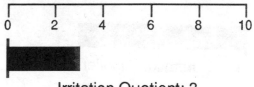

Irritation Quotient: 3

You don't know *what* that stuff on the floor is. Day-old cola? Used chewing gum? Or possibly a *present* from the kid who got sick during the last showing. Justice would be served if the usher who was supposed to clean between showings had to taste-test the gunk!

PEOPLE WHO LIGHT UP RIGHT AFTER THE "NO SMOKING" TRAILER ENDS.

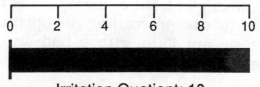

Irritation Quotient: 10

The first Bo Derek irritation in this study: a perfect 10.

There is no reason to tolerate this completely sub-human form of sewage. It's definitely "get-the-manager" time. 'Nuff said.

PEOPLE WHO, RIGHT BEFORE THE PICTURE STARTS, SIT DIRECTLY IN FRONT OF YOU WHEN THERE ARE HUNDREDS OF SEATS AVAILABLE.

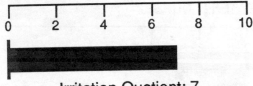

Irritation Quotient: 7

These are people who don't believe in one of the basic laws of nonverbal communication: Strangers occupying a theater will sit as far away from each other as possible.

Ignorance of the law is no excuse, either.

When this happens to you, you're not thinking about nonverbal laws. You just get upset because you can no longer see the screen.

There are two solutions. Either *you* move, to the seat directly in front of them just as the movie starts. Or, just begin reading the opening credits of the movie out loud with a bad stutter. That usually gets *them* to move.

PROJECTIONISTS WHO DON'T REALIZE THE FILM IS OUT OF FOCUS UNTIL THE END OF THE FIRST REEL.

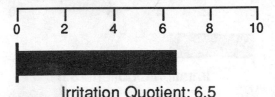

Irritation Quotient: 6.5

When it finally comes time to *watch* the movie, there is nothing more annoying than viewing a motion picture which is slightly out of focus.

After a minute or two has gone by and no correction is made, there will be one vocal individual who shouts out the one-word command, *"Focus!"*

Unfortunately, Mr. Union Projection Man has gone back to his snooze until the next 20-minute alarm goes off, at which time he'll start the next reel and finally hear the screaming chorus of *"Focus! Focus!"* from below.

Then he'll adjust the projector slightly and mumble about his job and how badly he's treated and how a strike is the only answer ... just before he nods off again.

Meanwhile, you're stuck watching blurred cinematic images you laid out six or seven bucks for.

PEOPLE WHO READ FOREIGN MOVIE SUBTITLES OUT LOUD.

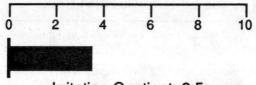

Irritation Quotient: 3.5

This phenomenon usually induces laughter from Superior People the first few times it occurs. It's funny to hear someone recite subtitles more or less to himself, because this person obviously can't comprehend the meaning by reading silently. (This is the same type of person whose lips move when he reads a book.)

Amusement quickly gives way to annoyance, however, when the person performs *every* subtitle that comes up, including simple ones like "Oh, yes!" and "Go!"

A dirty look usually quells this minor hackle uprising. If not, turn around a scrawl a few subtitles on his shirt with an ink pen.

USHERS WHO PATROL THE AISLES WITH A FLASHLIGHT, USUALLY AT A CRUCIAL POINT IN THE FILM.

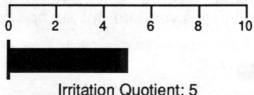

Irritation Quotient: 5

We've been hammering on the audience members so much, we've nearly forgotten about the direct negative effects theater employees can have on Superior Patrons.

Some theater ushers — like patrolmen on the beat — feel they have to make a quota of busts or else they'll be demoted to floor-sweeping duty. So, every now and then you'll see one of them wielding his trusty flashlight like a billy club, looking for people who put their feet on the backs of the seats.

Isn't it funny how they manage to shine that 200-watt floodlight in your eyes right when you're most engrossed in the story? It would be a lot funnier if you whipped out a pocket mirror and reflected the blinding light right back into *their* eyes.

PEOPLE WHO LEAVE TEN MINUTES BEFORE THE END OF A GOOD MOVIE.

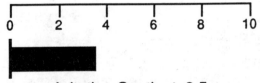

Irritation Quotient: 3.5

This behavior is beyond comprehension because *no* Superior would even *consider* exiting before the movie ends — *ever!* Even if the city was on fire or there was an air raid, they would stay until the end.

Seeing people leaving early from a concert is irking, but not nearly as much as watching them leave a theater prematurely. Don't these people care how the picture ends? How the plot resolves? Why did they bother coming at all? Unless it's a horrendous film or they discover they're bleeding to death, they've got no business vacating the theater.

If they refuse to adopt this sacred philosophy, they shouldn't be there in the first place,and should have their picture taken by an usher in the lobby, identifying them as someone who will forever be barred from seeing a movie in that theater again.

PEOPLE WHO STAND UP TO LEAVE DURING THE END CREDITS ... IN FRONT OF *YOU.*

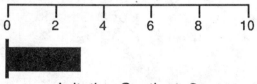

Irritation Quotient: 3

Another major requirement of being a Superior Person is to treat every life experience as an enriching one.

Staying to read the credits at the end of a film will have an enriching effect on you, the movie-goer. Individuals who take the trouble to read end credits are exciting, vital people who have an insatiable thirst for knowledge.

People who *don't* stay for the closing credits are not only rude and ignorant, but they sufficiently block your view of the screen while they stand there, deciding which fire exit to use.

Even though irritation may be inevitable in this situation, you should still continue to watch the credits until they are completely finished. Besides the above reasons, you'll also end up getting out of the empty parking lot in a flash.

* * *

It's interesting to see what ordeals people will endure to be amused. Like at amusement _parks_, for example. Some of the things that go on at these places between rides and attractions make you wonder if they really shouldn't call 'em _be_musement parks...

CATEGORY #10:
AMUSEMENT PARKS

(Step Right Up and Win Some Crap!)

An amusement park is a great measurer of maturity.

It is a place that changes very little, if at all, while it exists. Yet, it's not uncommon for adults who go to the amusement park to have been the kids who were there 20 and 30 years ago. Now, perhaps they have kids of their own to bring or maybe they're newly in love and go to the park to be romantic with their sweetheart.

Regardless of how long you've been going to your local amusement park, it is a universal constant that the older you get, the less tolerant you are of things going on within the gates. In extreme cases, the fast rides you loved as a kid now make your stomach turn or your back hurt. In more common cases, the lines you once sprinted to get into are now approached with lead feet at the thought of waiting 45 minutes for a 90-second thrill. The souvenirs you were excited to win as a child are now obvious rip-offs when you consider how much cash you have to lay out to win one — maybe. The enthusiasm to stay until midnight now begins to wane around 6:30, right after dinner.

The amusement park is a perfect example of why you start a family. When the hassles start outweighing the fun, you have kids so *they* can have fun and you won't carry the burden of having it all yourself. Living vicariously through your children starts to become a parental pastime.

However, even though the responsibility of fun is now on your offsprings' shoulders, the irritating aspects of the park are still on yours (just like it was for *your* parents). Here then, are several amusement park-style annoyances which would ruin any Superior Person's day (parent or otherwise):

DISCOVERING YOUR FAVORITE RIDE HAS BEEN TORN DOWN.

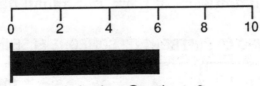

Irritation Quotient: 6

One of the great rites of passage into adulthood is when you go to the amusement park and rush to brave the ride you've gone on first ever since you were a little kid. About 100 feet away from where it should be, you stop short and your jaw drops. "Your Ride" is no longer there. They took it away. They didn't just move it, *they tore it down.*

Without your permission. And all you can do is stand there in stupefaction.

Welcome to the jungle. Your totally innocent "fun" attitude toward this place will never be the same. You are now an embittered Superior Adult.

PEOPLE WHO PAY 20 DOLLARS ADMISSION, AND THE FIRST THING THEY DO IS SPEND *MORE* MONEY PLAYING VIDEO GAMES.

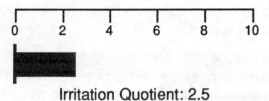

Irritation Quotient: 2.5

Curiously, you will notice as you walk through the park on your way to your first ride of the day, people in the arcades playing video games. You look at your watch and it's 10:02 AM — the park has just opened. Why are these people starting off their day spending *more* money?? Get on a ride! This is an amusement park, not a mall hangout!

PEOPLE WHO CUT IN FRONT OF SOMEONE ELSE IN LINE.

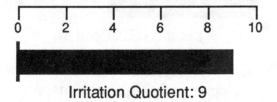

Irritation Quotient: 9

You know this one all too well. It doesn't even have to be you the jerk cuts in front of — the result is the same. That's another 30 seconds you'll have to wait to get into your Kadillac Kar or Log-Shaped Boat.

And that limp-wristed warning sign by the park admission booth is a joke: "Line-jumping and cutting are cause for removal from the park." Who are they kidding? Have you ever seen a single park employee enforce that law? Of course not. They just sit by the line entrance with their 48-inch-high measuring stick, ready to bust midget infiltrators.

PEOPLE WHO *LET* OTHER PEOPLE CUT IN LINE.

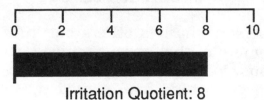

Irritation Quotient: 8

These morons are just as infuriating as the ones who do the actual cutting because they treat the whole procedure like some *Mission: Impossible* operation.

This is the guy who is ahead of you in line, but is turned to *face* you. First you believe he's staring at you, but it soon becomes apparent he's searching for someone or something on the midway.

After a couple of minutes avoiding eye contact, you wonder what the hell he's looking for. Realization sets in when he starts wildly signaling for his buddies (who had been at the Frozen Banana stand) to join him in line. They do, and this act then gives way to the main line-cutting irritation.

95

The best place for this to happen is in the line for the bumper cars, 'cause once you get on the ride, you *know* who your ramming target is, and you will take *no* prisoners.

SWIVEL-HEADED PEOPLE WHO NEVER NOTICE THE LINE IS MOVING IN FRONT OF THEM.

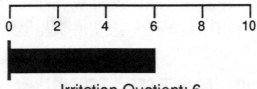

Irritation Quotient: 6

The person who lets others cut in line is frequently guilty of this absent-minded act as well. He's so busy looking for his pals, he never sees the mile-long gap which has opened up in the line ahead of him.

Anybody whose head is constantly swiveling left and right is bound to miss the rhythmic pattern of the advancing queue. Evidently, achieving the goal of standing in line (getting on the ride) is not as important to this person as checking out the chick with the cute butt or leering at the bodybuilder with the tank-top.

COUPLES WHO PRACTICE HEAVY PETTING WHILE WAITING IN LINE.

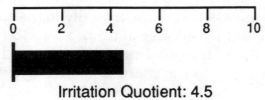

Irritation Quotient: 4.5

It doesn't require a sharp eye to observe that many sexually insatiable couples like to go to amusement parks. They can be seen in almost every line, sucking each others' faces down their throats. While some of the action is almost as good as the stuff you can rent from the back room of your local video store, there are two reasons why this exhibitionistic practice becomes rapidly riling:

1) To have all this fondling and salivating constantly in your line of vision gets real old real quick.

2) Most of the time, the participants in these public "how-to" displays are stunningly unattractive individuals, and it soon becomes akin to watching a freak show.

REFRESHMENT STANDS STRATEGICALLY LOCATED IN THE MIDDLE OF THE LINE FOR A RIDE.

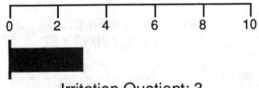

Irritation Quotient: 3

Ride lines move slowly enough without having to deal with impressionable people who see a stack of giant cola cups and decide they're suddenly parched.

The rest of the maze invariably waits with arms folded as these jokers get back change for the twenty they gave the vendor for one lousy cup.

Meanwhile a 500-foot chasm has opened up in the line in front of them.

97

Just blow on past them. Then pretend you don't recognize them when they catch up and say, "Uh, isn't this my spot?"

GETTING IN LINE BEHIND THE SAME OBNOXIOUS PEOPLE YOU WERE BEHIND FOR THE LAST RIDE.

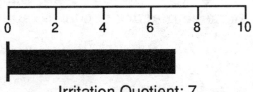

Irritation Quotient: 7

It's maddening because all of the unpleasant things already witnessed will occur all over again. In the case of getting behind the *same* offenders, however, you will get even more upset because you usually don't notice them until you've been in the "maze" for five minutes and cannot easily get out.

A RIDE WHICH SHUTS DOWN BECAUSE OF RAIN OR MALFUNCTION JUST WHEN YOU FINALLY REACH THE FRONT OF THE LINE.

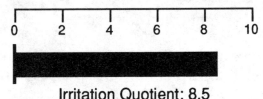

Irritation Quotient: 8.5

The last entry in the line-oriented irritations is indeed the final ignominy. After all the frustrations and thinly-veiled impatience at waiting over an hour to get on this stupid ride, it starts to rain which causes the contraption to shut down ... and since it's not natural to bring an umbrella to an amusement park, you get drenched.

TEENAGERS WHO VISIT AMUSEMENT PARKS WITH 35 OF THEIR FRIENDS.

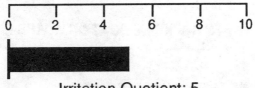

Irritation Quotient: 5

These are the same twerps who invade the front rows of movie theaters in force. They've picked up a few more acquaintances since then, however. How they all know each other is amazing in itself. How they all get on the same ride together is further stupefying.

PEOPLE WHO, IN 90-DEGREE HEAT, WILL STAND IN THE BLAZING SUN TO WATCH A MARCHING BAND.

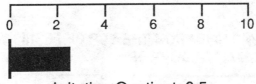

Irritation Quotient: 2.5

Totally amazing behavior! Dozens of people frozen in their tracks, rapidly developing heat stroke, watching a high school marching band from Anytown, U.S.A. blaring its thoroughly unmusical version of *The Hawaii Five-O Theme* is a remarkable sight to behold.

Many times you'll find yourself wanting to run up and slap a few of these zombies on the face to snap them out of their trance, but you're much too busy sitting in an air-conditioned restaurant or taking a splash on a water ride. One pictures these folks spending their Saturday afternoons at the airport watching planes take off.

KIDS WHO TRY TO ROCK THE BOAT ON WATER RIDES.

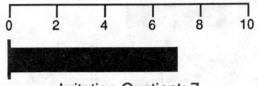

Irritation Quotient: 7

An activity that was a riot as a child becomes nerve-racking as an adult. You've got to wonder if these kids would attempt the rocking action on a real vessel in the middle of the ocean.

You can only hope these juvenile terrorists never join the Coast Guard, and are on duty the day your boat is sinking.

PEOPLE WHO SPIT FROM THE TOP OF FERRIS WHEELS OR OTHER HIGH-ALTITUDE RIDES.

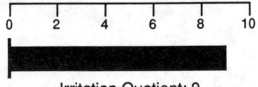

Irritation Quotient: 9

Snotty kids and certain immature adults find sadistic pleasure in creating their own "water rides" ... they spit a juicy hocker from the highest point of a ride and see who it hits on the ground below.

100

GOSH, I THOUGHT THE WATER RIDE WAS ON THE
OTHER SIDE OF THE PARK???

Witnessing someone perform this disgusting act rates an Irritation Quotient of 9. To be the *victim* of the spittle attack sends the reading off the scale.

Wouldn't it be sweet revenge if each amusement park had a firehose trained on the peak of the Ferris Wheel ride — and any spitter would immediately be doused with a quick twenty-gallon blast.

GETTING ON THE SKY RIDE WITH STRANGE KIDS WHO ENJOY HANGING OUT THE SIDE OF THE CAR.

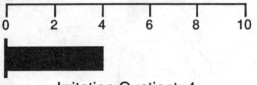

Irritation Quotient: 4

Disneyland has one of these. Many parks refer to theirs as the Sky Ride. It's the overhead bucket-like cars that travel along a steel cable from one end of the park to the other, mainly used for picturesque transportation.

Not content with the scenic aspect of the ride, some kids get on the bucket to hang out the side and rock it back and forth — much to the quiet panic of the Superior People who happen to be trapped inside with them. (While most Superiors don't have a fear of heights, they *do* have a fear of being flattened by the concrete below — it comes along with having a functional brain.)

* * *

After a long, annoying day at the amusement park, it's time to unwind at a nice, quiet restaurant.

Prepare yourself for a long, annoying <u>night</u>...

CATEGORY #11:

RESTAURANTS

(Disasters in Dining Out)

Unlike movie theaters, concert halls and amusement parks, a restaurant is a place where the patrons are *expected* to imitate civilized people. Except for the occasional wailing child, only a few distracting irritations originate from the customers. The others come from the restaurant staff (waiters, waitresses, busboys or order takers) and from the actual food that is served.

The following list contains everyday irritations to be found in both fast-food and sit-down restaurants.

FAST-FOOD ORDER-TAKERS WHO SAY, "CAN I TAKE YOUR ORDER?" THE MILLISECOND YOU SET FOOT IN THE DOOR.

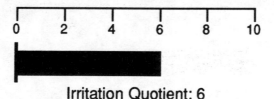

Irritation Quotient: 6

This happens quite often these days, and it's to the point of being a huge joke among the employees as opposed to being a matter of super-friendly service. They try to see how worked up they can

104

get you by giving you the feeling that *they're* in a hurry, too.

Sometimes you can see them waiting for you as soon as you get out of your car and head for the entrance. The place isn't busy and they can smell a burger customer a kilometer away. You'd think they were working on commission, the way they accost you as soon as you step through the doorway.

It may be a fast-food joint and you may have come here 200 times before, but you still have the right to check out the menu to see if, by some miracle, there is actually something new available.

Next time a burger-slapper pops that inevitable question too early, ask him what he recommends and have him go into descriptive detail as to the ingredients of each item. Then, when he's finished, order a cup of water (hold the ice) and go to another restaurant. The satisfaction gained will be worth the extra trip.

CUSTOMERS WHO SAY "TO GO" WHEN ORDERING, THEN SIT IN THE DINING AREA TO EAT.

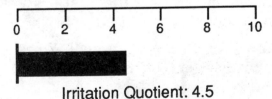

Irritation Quotient: 4.5

A lot of classless people make this practice a regular habit, and it should aggravate the hell out of any Superiors worth their salt (or other seasoning). You know the kind: He says his order is "to go," then he and his take-out bag nonchalantly slip into the dining room to eat, all to save five or six cents (In some states there is no sales tax on "To Go" food orders.).

At this point, Superiors fantasize about two-dark-suited gentlemen entering to announce they are Fast Food Feds, then proceed to roughly escort the offender to a holding area for ten hours of questioning.

SUPPOSEDLY CLEAN SILVERWARE WITH BITS OF FOOD ON IT.

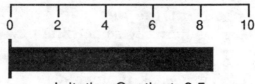

Irritation Quotient: 8.5

Get on the phone to the Board of Health and the FDA pronto and shut that bistro down! Silverware that looks like somebody was using it to pick his nose can be thoroughly enraging as well as unhealthy.

Then again, it's undoubtedly been through the dishwasher, so the food that's still stuck on it is probably thoroughly sterilized.

Go ahead and use the utensil. You can always sue somebody later.

SALAD BARS THAT HAVE SNEEZE-GUARDS WHICH ARE ACTUALLY USED.

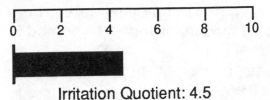

Irritation Quotient: 4.5

As you stand at the salad bar, there's nothing quite as unappetizing as seeing someone's expelled sneeze residue on that Plexiglas sanitary cover. The fact that someone felt obliged to use it is enough to make you look around and double-check to be sure if you *really* want to dine in Chéz Botulism.

SALAD BARS THAT FEATURE "AGED" VEGETABLES WHICH HAVE TAKEN ROOT.

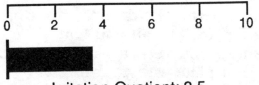

Irritation Quotient: 3.5

Okay, you've decided to stay despite the solidified sneeze directly in front of you. You dip the plastic tongs into the lettuce and notice most of the leaves are a disgusting shade of orange.

Bypassing the lettuce, you go for the onions ... oh, but they have visible roots growing out of the sides of the container. You size up the rest of the salad ingredients with a quick glance and it becomes clear these veggies were last replaced about a month ago. Seeing the partially green Cheddar cheese convinces you to return to your seat and brave the main course.

Don't turn around as you walk. You might see the mutated food following right behind you.

PEOPLE WHO DRINK THE REMAINING DRESSING FROM THEIR SALAD BOWL.

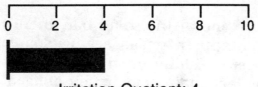

Irritation Quotient: 4

One of the all-time dining stomach-turners, it's amazing how you'll look up from your meal just in time to witness someone (usually a man) slurping his salad bowl to get every last drop of tasty dressing. Ecccch!

The worst part is, he doesn't care who sees him and when he does it, all you can do is marvel at his crassness and return to cleaning the steak sauce off your plate with your finger.

OBNOXIOUS "THEME MUSIC" IN SPECIALTY RESTAURANTS.

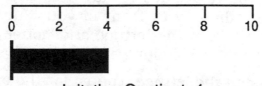

Irritation Quotient: 4

Mexican restaurants are prime annoyers in this area.

Have you ever listened to one Herb Alpert & the Tijuana Brass song repeatedly for 2 hours? No? Go to almost any Mexican restaurant and you'll know what it's like.

Hearing 120 or more continuous minutes of harmonizing trumpets while digging into your fajitas is enough to drive even Chi Chi Rodriguez around the bend.

RESTAURANTS WHICH FEATURE MANDATORY VALET PARKING.

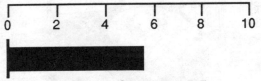

Irritation Quotient: 5.5

Eating at fancy-shmancy restaurants which feature monkey-suited college kids parking your car for you may be a sign of prestige and status, but to any Superior it's a source of stress from the minute they get out of the car with the engine still running.

Why can't people park their own cars? Why is there a need for daredevils hot-rodding around the parking lot with *your* vehicle? Will you ever see your car again in the condition you left it? Does your insurance cover damage done by strange drivers in a restaurant lot? Are those kids making duplicates of your keys while you're eating dinner?

The stress gets worse if you happen to own a vehicle which qualifies as a "beater." Going to a fancy restaurant and emerging from your rusted-out bomb in formal wear elicits sarcastic snickers and comments from the valets. They immediately know you don't do this very often and that you probably don't earn much more annually than they do.

And to top it all off, you're supposed to tip them for taking a joyride in your car!

If valet parking is mandatory, it should also be mandatory that the valets wash and wax your vehicle while you're having dinner. At least this would justify their tip.

RESTAURANTS WHOSE MENUS LIST COMMON, EVERYDAY DISHES ... WHICH YOU LATER DISCOVER CONTAIN STRANGE INGREDIENTS THAT DON'T BELONG IN THERE AT ALL.

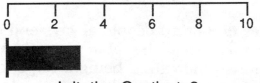

Irritation Quotient: 3

An example which causes picky Superior Eaters all kinds of agitation is the following type of menu selection:

Seven jumbo fantail shrimp (so far so good),

Marinated in butter and garlic (sounds tasty),

Served in a wine sauce (yum!)

Sounds delicious! What could go wrong, huh? So you order the shrimp and it comes to your table just like you pictured it in your mind ... except it's topped with almonds. Or water chestnuts ... or anything else out of left field which totally negates your appetite. And what really grabs you is the fact that the menu didn't inform you about that extra, incongruous ingredient!

That's why you've got to be very careful when ordering in many fancy restaurants, because you might just get your veal marinated in liver bile sauce, or your baked chicken wrapped in squirrel fur.

LARGE PARTIES OF PEOPLE SITTING IN CLOSE PROXIMITY WHO INSIST ON SHOUTING AT EACH OTHER.

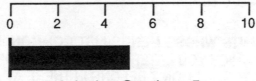

Irritation Quotient: 5

Parties of 8 or 10 people always end up yelling at each other across the table when they converse. And you just know that, being a Superior Person, you'll end up being seated at a table right next to them. And why? Because you can take it, that's why ... even though the loudness often gets so distracting, you start missing your mouth with your silverware.

PEOPLE WHO SHAMELESSLY SMOKE IN NON-SMOKING SECTIONS.

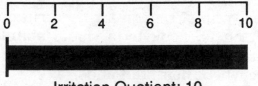

Irritation Quotient: 10

Of all the restaurant irritations, this is by far the worst. You didn't shell out hard-earned money to sit in this over-priced restaurant and try to enjoy your meal with someone else's cigarette smoke wafting in your face.

Like smoking in movie theaters, this practice shows blatant disregard for rules, human rights and now, laws. This infraction should most certainly be punishable by a life sentence in a 6-by-6, windowless, smoke-filled room with no ventilation. The only thing worse than a person who ignores the non-smoking law in restaurants is the restaurant that does not enforce that law.

HAVING TO ORDER YOUR STEAK EXTRA WELL-DONE IN ORDER TO HAVE IT SERVED MEDIUM-RARE.

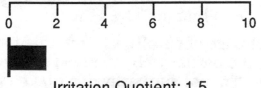

Irritation Quotient: 1.5

You know all too well that when you order a steak anywhere but in the finest restaurants, you better order it burned, just to make sure it's served to you at least medium-rare.

The fact that you have to remember this steak rule is the "prime" reason for the irritation. Many so-called "chefs" cook by a visual standard: if it looks okay, serve it. The timer is only used to determine when their shift ends.

WAITERS/WAITRESSES WHO POUNCE ON YOU TO ASK HOW EVERYTHING IS ... THE MOMENT YOU HAVE A MOUTHFUL OF FOOD.

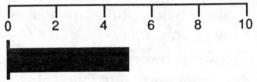

Irritation Quotient: 5

This is an annoying habit which waiters and waitresses have been practicing for decades.

They hide behind a potted plant or in an alcove where they can observe you eating. Then, at a given moment, they scurry up to your table and ask, "Is everything alright?" A veteran server will have timed the question perfectly: You'll have a mouthful of entree and all you can do is nod or mutter, "Mmm-hmmm."

As a change of pace, next time this happens to you, spit the partially-chewed food into your palm and reply, "I'm not sure, why don't *you* try a bite?"

BUSBOYS WHO PARK THEIR CARTS NEXT TO YOU WHILE THEY CLEAR OFF OTHER TABLES.

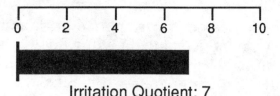

Irritation Quotient: 7

Certain less-ritzy bistros feature busboys who put dirty dishes and leftover food into little roll-around carts. If you're a particularly unlucky Superior Person, these busboys will pick up on that fact and park their carts next to your table while they clear off other places.

It is indeed disgusting to eat your meal right beside a load of half-eaten-food-encrusted plates, yet there is some compelling internal force which makes you want to look inside the cart (similar to covering your eyes during a horror movie, but peeking through your fingers because you just *have* to see what's happening). This urge can't be explained but it must be fought, otherwise it could have an adverse effect on your digestive system.

PEOPLE WHO ASK TO TASTE FOOD OFF YOUR PLATE.

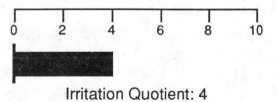

Irritation Quotient: 4

Pretty gauche behavior from a person who should be on "Lifestyles of the Mooch and Famished."

Anybody besides your spouse or date who asks if they can have some of your food should be carried off by a Soylent Green truck and made into a biscuit. The same goes with folks who brashly inquire if they can have a sip from your glass, bottle or can.

You don't always know where those lips have been. So just stand pat and refuse. You may offend the individual, but you'll still have your health.

WAITERS/WAITRESSES WHO STAND THERE WATCHING YOU FILL IN THE TIP COLUMN OF YOUR CREDIT CARD SLIP.

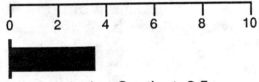

Irritation Quotient: 3.5

Superior Diners who use a credit card to pay for their meals know what an aggravation this can be. A server who watches you decide how big a tip to leave is being just plain rude.

When this happens, follow this rule of thumb: Don't write anything and see how long it takes the server to get the message and leave. For every second he or she loiters, subtract a dime from the gratuity (a quarter for checks over 30 dollars).

The experience your server gains from this treatment will be valued for a long time to come.

* * *

Did you know that when dining in a restaurant, the indigestion you suffer usually is a result of the ambience and the servers, not the food? Did you know that when you dine anywhere else, the <u>opposite</u> is usually true?

Food for thought...

CATEGORY #12:
FOOD

(Eat, Drink and Be Harried)

Many Superiors are notoriously picky eaters. Unless they have complete control over what goes into their meal, they can get quite nervous about what might be served them.

That's why restaurants are not the only food-serving establishments they approach with trepidation: Friends' and relatives' homes, banquet halls, wedding receptions, testimonial dinners and other places where strangers prepare the grub cause SPs much anxiety.

Here we examine food-oriented irritations which can present themselves no matter where you dine.

WEIRD VEGETABLES WHICH CALL TO MIND THE AROMA OF BABIES' DIAPERS.

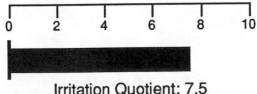

Irritation Quotient: 7.5

Salads are very "in" these days. Especially popular are dark green vegetables which are rich sources of vitamins.

Regardless of what is or isn't good for you, different people will always like different types of food, and the same goes for various varieties of veggies. Still, there are some vegetables which will induce gags from the majority of SPs because they smell and/or taste like some sort of human waste material.

The following veggies, while good for your health, have a very bad effect on your olfactory nerve and taste buds:

Eggplant

Zucchini

Brussel Sprouts

Beets

Cauliflower

Turnips

Swiss Chard

Trying to disguise the rank flavor of these infernal foodstuffs with condiments or seasonings in order to painlessly get their nutrients won't work, either. These vegetables are testaments to the old adage, "No pain, no gain."

EXCESS SILK LEFT IN CORN-ON-THE-COB.

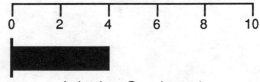

Irritation Quotient: 4

Sloppy corn-huskers are responsible for the distraction of encountering strand after strand of silk as you munch on your corn-on-the-cob.

Corn-on-the-cob is delicious, and the last thing you want to do while you're eating it is continuously pull a bunch of hair-like things out of your teeth. Contrary to what some inferior people must think, cornsilk is not built-in dental floss.

RUBBERIZED KETCHUP THAT FORMS AROUND THE LIP OF THE BOTTLE.

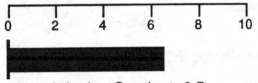

Irritation Quotient: 6.5

This is an unpleasant sight resulting from some lazy person failing to wipe the mouth of the ketchup bottle after using it.

The red stuff drools down over the lip, the cap is replaced, then four days later you open the bottle again and voila! Rubber ketchup.

It's disgusting and irritating to encounter this while preparing to dig into a burger and fries. As therapy, peel off the mutated condiment, place it in an envelope and mail it anonymously to the person who caused it to form.

CREAM-OF-ANYTHING SOUP.

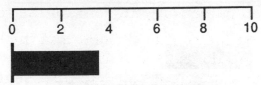

Irritation Quotient: 3.5

Unless it's home-made, cream of _____ soup (you fill in the blank) is something to avoid at all costs. You don't know *what* foreign matter the cream is camouflaging.

It almost reminds one of warmed-over infant regurgitant.

DRINKING OUT OF A CAN AND TASTING THE ALUMINUM.

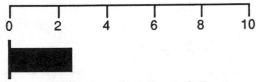

Irritation Quotient: 2.5

When you're thirsty and you can't wait to slurp down a can of your favorite cola or lemonade, you don't want and certainly don't *expect* to be tasting the metal that holds the liquid.

Yet, that's what often happens. The unappetizing flavor of aluminum overpowers the pop you're drinking and turns your taste buds inside out.

However, if you actually *like* the taste of metal, you should drink it along with a sandwich of nuts and bolts on rye.

121

THE LEAKY BOTTOMS OF ICE CREAM CONES.

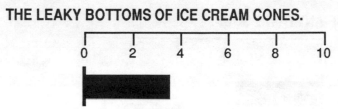

Irritation Quotient: 3.5

They can put a man on the moon and they can take photographs of Neptune, but they can't make a sugar ice cream cone that doesn't leak from the bottom tip.

This stress-inducer grows a little stronger if you happen to forget these cones regularly drip, and you end up getting melted ice cream droplets on your new shirt or blouse in front of your new date.

NOT BEING ABLE TO DIG OUT THE RESIDUAL FOOD FROM THE BOTTOM OF BOTTLES AND CONTAINERS.

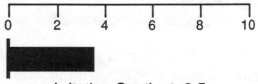

Irritation Quotient: 3.5

Superior "Joe Consumer" isn't what you'd call cheap, but he does like to get his money's worth. That means he intensely *dis*likes anything that remotely amounts to "waste," especially when it comes to edibles.

And you know what *that* means.

In diametric opposition to this attitude, there is an unspoken motto among food-industry people that goes something like this: "We must see to it that Joe Consumer cannot possibly, no matter how frantically he tries, get every bit of food or drop of liquid out of our containers."

This creed applies to condiment bottles with openings so small, you can't fit a spoon through it to scrape out the remaining product.

It particularly applies to many pre-packaged pudding and yogurt containers, which for some reason feature bottoms with intricate, maze-like recesses that prevent you from digging out all the food! You can try using a spoon, a fork, a screwdriver... but you'll never get it all!

When this irritation gets to be too much for you, write a letter to the only person who can help — consumer advocate David Horowitz — demanding he start an investigation into who is behind this container-crevice conspiracy!

THE BLACK BOTTOM OF LITER-SIZE SOFT DRINK BOTTLES.

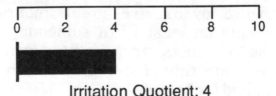

Irritation Quotient: 4

During what executive soda meeting was it decided that the majority of liter-size soft drink bottles will feature black bottoms?

If this container happens to hold cola or root beer, the black bottom can often be mistaken for the liquid itself. Although completely empty, this bottle in the refrigerator gives the impression that there is still pop left in it.

This then causes great anguish and confusion for the next Superior who retrieves the bottle to have a cool drink, only to find the proverbial well to be empty. He or she then yells at the spouse or the kids, the family eventually breaks up and before long, the entire American social system is in a shambles.

All this damage because some bored soft drink executive (probably the boss's son) one day decided to make his pop bottle bottoms basic black.

DISCOVERING IT WOULD HAVE TAKEN LESS TIME TO PREPARE SOMETHING IN THE CONVENTIONAL OVEN INSTEAD OF THE MICROWAVE.

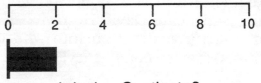

Irritation Quotient: 2

Microwave ovens are great technological advancements (at least until someone discovers they cause liver spots, or something worse). Still, there are some things a regular oven can do quicker ... and/or better.

Like making hot chocolate. By the time you nuke the milk in the microwave for 45 seconds eight different times, and turn the cup and stir the milk a few times, cows have become extinct and you'll have to drink black coffee from now on. The old stove top gives it to you with little hassle and in only three or four minutes.

The microwave oven makes frozen pizzas come out soggy. Toaster ovens produce crisp, tasty ones after only a little more time, and you don't have to stop in the middle of cooking to turn it clockwise 45.73628364 degrees.

HAVING DINNER AT THE HOME OF IN-LAWS OR YOUR BOSS AND FEELING OBLIGED TO EAT FOOD *YOU* CAN'T STAND, BUT WHICH *THEY* HAVE SLAVED OVER ALL DAY.

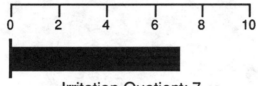

Irritation Quotient: 7

Don't you hate it when you have to be polite out of necessity rather than desire?

You're a guest for dinner. The hosts are beaming big time about the meal they've prepared, and you, of course, are hungry. Unfortunately, what they bring to the table is a steaming heap of something you can't stomach ... like Eggplant Casserole or goat liver soufflé ... followed by chocolate covered insects (alive and squiggling!)

They could have asked you or your spouse or your date what kinds of food you liked beforehand, but no. *They* like what they've prepared, therefore *everybody* in the world must like it!

IT'S AN OLD FAMILY RECIPE FOR GALL BLADDER PIE
— AND DON'T WORRY, THERE'S PLENTY MORE
WHEN YOU'RE FINISHED WITH THAT!

Bad attitude, bad dinner, bad evening. And unless you really are into hurting peoples' pride, try eating the stuff without breathing through your nose. This way, you won't be able to taste it. It'll just feel weird in your mouth.

CONVERSING WITH SOMEONE WHO HAS FOOD WEDGED BETWEEN HIS/HER TEETH.

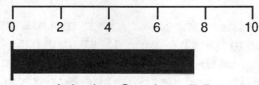

Irritation Quotient: 7.5

One of the great squeamish irritations is having to keep eye contact with someone who has a food *grossiosity* jammed in his or her dental work. No matter how much you shift in your chair or try not to stare at his mouth, the irritation will not go away.

And you never know if you should tell the guy about his embarrassing problem, hand him a toothpick or just keep your trap shut. But don't you know, this guy usually enjoys smiling and laughing a lot, exposing his modified choppers for everyone else to see.

* * *

The basic necessity of "food" is a big reason all us humans are impersonally referred to as "consumers." And your basic "consumer" ... otherwise known as "shopper" ... is another big reason Superiors get a little crazier every day ...

127

CATEGORY #13:
SHOPPING
(Mall of the Wild)

Yet another necessary evil in this lightning-paced world is the act of shopping. Between keeping up with the Joneses and staying ahead of the Smiths and getting the latest gadget and stocking up on those familiar grocery items, shopping has developed into a strange recreational activity for many humans.

Because of this, the social phenomenon called "shopping" coaxes many ILFs (Inferior Life Forms) out of the woodwork, and only Superior Persons seem to notice them enough to be irked by them.

We'll examine the "greatest hits" of browsing bugaboos. Most of these galling items involve other shoppers or store employees but, like the other categories in this book, a few involve those damned inanimate objects. They are divided into two sub-categories:

A) General Shopping ... which deals with the physical act of shopping.

B) Shopping Malls ... which concentrates on that unique, enclosed cultural vacuum.

128

GENERAL SHOPPING

A CUSTOMER WHO THINKS YOU WORK IN THE STORE YOU ARE BOTH SHOPPING IN.

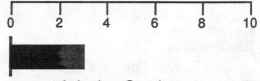

Irritation Quotient: 3

Have you ever been intently combing the shelves for your brand of shampoo or toothpaste and suddenly hear a voice say, "Do you have anymore of that mouthwash you had on sale?"

As a Superior Person, you will react one of two ways:

1) You'll be insulted at the notion that this low-life thinks your clothes resemble those of a monkey-suited stockperson.

2) You'll be piqued by this complete stranger breaking your concentration.

Either way, turn to him or her and reply, "Do you always talk to yourself?" The amount of kindness or coldness you put in your voice is totally up to you.

FINALLY BUYING AN APPLIANCE AFTER WEEKS OF COMPARISON-SHOPPING, ONLY TO FIND IT FOR A LOT LESS MONEY IN THE NEXT STORE YOU VISIT.

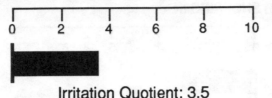

Irritation Quotient: 3.5

Here's one of those inanimate-object irritations that can actually happen with any item you might purchase. Appliances, however, are generally bought once in a great while and can be expensive, so the effect is more gut-wrenching.

After weeks of searching and deciding between various makes and models, you finally buy one you like — and hey, it's even on sale! What a smart consumer you are!

Not smart enough, though, because on the way home you run into Al's Generic Drug Store to pick up some dental floss and you stumble upon an entire aisle full of the appliance you just bought ... for 25 dollars less than the "sale" price you just paid.

As you seethe, you reason that you *could* buy this one and take the other one back, but that means you'll only find it somewhere else for still less money, and the game would begin again. The best thing to do is keep the one you purchased. You'll save gas money and you will only get *that* mad once.

That is, until you buy your next appliance.

STORES THAT ARE "CONVENIENTLY" OUT OF AN ADVERTISED ITEM THE FIRST TEN MINUTES OF THE SALE.

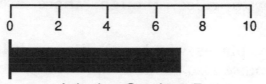

0   2   4   6   8   10

Irritation Quotient: 7

Discount department stores are notorious for this. You go in specifically to buy that 4-for-a-dollar soap which was advertised in your Sunday newspaper supplement, only to find the store is "already out of it," or "the shipment's stuck on a highway somewhere in Montana."

Then the clerk tells you to go up to the service desk for a rain check. And you walk up there, simmering all the way, knowing full well you can't wash your face with a rain check.

STORES WITH THE ATTITUDE THAT THEY ARE "DOING YOU A FAVOR" BY BEING IN BUSINESS.

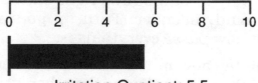

0   2   4   6   8   10

Irritation Quotient: 5.5

Have you ever shopped in a store where the employees make you feel like you should thank *them* for being open for business? This is a Do-You-a-Favor Store.

Most stores' basic philosophy toward customer relations is simple: Please the customer, make him

131

or her feel welcome, charge a fair price and chances are, they will be back.

As with rules, though, there are always exceptions.

Many places which sell hip, with-it, trendy merchandise also adopt a hip, with-it, trendy attitude toward their customers — arrogance. Many clothing stores, record stores and independently-owned specialty shops blatantly cop a "what are *you* doing here?" air when you step through the door. According to their employees' actions and facial expressions, they are doing *you* a tremendous service by being in business in the first place, and by offering the items they stock at jacked-up prices. They disapprove of you browsing too long (however long that is), and are generally sullen and rude if you *dare* to ask one of them a question, or perhaps they'll answer you in a "you mean you didn't *know* that??" tone of voice.

If it's at all possible, you should storm out of a Do-You-a-Favor Store with disgust on your face, or at the very least, be rude right back at the hip, with-it, trendy offender. Turn up *your* nose and comment how *passé* everything is.

No matter how much the management thinks you need them, it is *always* the other way around, and sooner or later when their doors close forever, they'll realize that fact.

TRYING TO NONCHALANTLY RENT A PORNO VIDEO WHILE TWELVE CHILDREN ARE IN THE STORE.

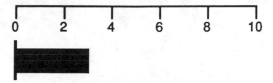

Irritation Quotient: 3

Come on, own up to it, you liberal Superiors. How many of you have ever rented a porno video? (Not *bought*, because if you *bought* a porno video, you wasted your money.)

A lot of people rent porno videos for reasons other than to de-yawn a bachelor party. They do it because it adds variety and fun to a romance and (more importantly) 99 per cent of them are hilariously awful.

But the main difficulty in securing a porno video occurs in the public act of renting. Most mainstream video stores have their "adult" cassettes in a back room behind some sort of foreboding door. So, when you go in the back, you can't browse too long because the customers and employees out front will begin to wonder just what you're doing with yourself. You must know what you want, get the tape box and unobtrusively head for the counter.

Here is where the real problem starts. By now there are twelve or fifteen kids in the store watching *Master Warlords of the Cosmos* which the store shows every afternoon on its large-screen TV. The kids may be strangers to each other but they have one thing in common: They all saw *you* (synonyms: pervert, voyeur, deviant) stroll out of the Dirty Movie Room.

133

You nonchalantly avoid all eye-contact and take your explicit triple-X cassette box to the counter where — ten times out of eleven — the clerk is a kid as well. By now you're burning up and thinking, "Why me?" Meanwhile, the clerk kid perpetuates the awkwardness by taking his good old time writing up the bill.

Besides all this discomfort, the clerk kid has taken your name and address, so now he and his pals know where you live. You are now positive they'll stop by tonight and peek into your window to find out why you rented "Debbie Does the NFL, the NBA, and Every Bowler Named 'Al'."

DEPARTMENT STORE EMPLOYEES WHO NAG YOU TO USE YOUR CREDIT CARD WHEN YOU WANT TO PAY CASH.

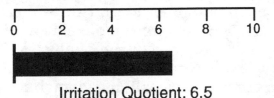

Irritation Quotient: 6.5

You know, you don't have to have your credit card with you anymore to pay by charge in department stores. Clerks will gladly look up your account number in order to assist you in paying by plastic.

If you tell a store associate you're purchasing an item with cash, it's to the point where she'll snort and give you a dirty look. "Caaaash?? Wouldn't you rather pay by charge??"

What, is money being phased out? What's wrong with cash?

Here's what's wrong with cash: The store can't demand a monthly finance charge from you on a cash payment!

PEOPLE WHO WATCH FOOTBALL GAMES ON STORE TELEVISIONS.

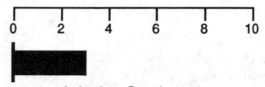

Irritation Quotient: 3

Now, a baffler for you.

Go into any Sears and Roebuck on any Sunday afternoon between September and January and you will find several, possibly dozens of people (mostly men) standing around the TV sets in the Electronics Department, completely engrossed in a football game to the exclusion of all else. If the TVs happen to be across the aisle from the Furniture Department, observe all the armchair quarterbacks making themselves right at home in the mock living room displays.

Why are these people there? Don't they have homes? Are their *own* television sets in disrepair? Are they so henpecked that they are forced to accompany their wives to the store and shop with them? If so, why aren't the wives forcing the guys to *stay* with them as well? As it is, they would have been better off leaving the deadbeats at home! And why don't department store managers kick these bums out for loitering? Tantalizing questions, all.

KIDS WHO RUN THE WRONG WAY ON ESCALATORS.

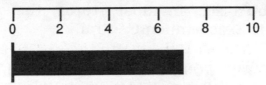

Irritation Quotient: 7

Escalators ought to be featured attractions at amusement parks, since kids love to ride them and make life miserable for Superior Shoppers who use them, too.

These brats, later in life, get their thrills by driving the wrong way down freeway exit ramps.

CASHIERS WHO INSTANTLY BECOME SLOW AND STUPID THE MOMENT YOU GET IN LINE.

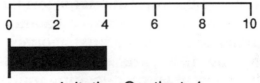

Irritation Quotient: 4

A cashier's job is to keep the checkout line as short as possible. Your job as a shopper is to get *in* the shortest line possible. Sounds like a good system, right? Right, but it's at this point that something goes horribly wrong. The minute you enter a line, the cashier suddenly forgets what is on sale or how to ring up a charge or how to prevent the cash register from going TILT.

Your aggravation increases by what kind of hurry you're in divided by how apologetic the cashier appears. Usually she's not apologetic at all. In fact, most of the time she could easily be a representative from a Do-You-a-Favor Store.

As you'll see, in most stores, the checkout counter is Exasperation Central.

CASHIERS WHO WON'T BELIEVE AN OBVIOUSLY HONEST PERSON WHEN HE/SHE TELLS THEM THE PRICE OF AN UNMARKED ITEM.

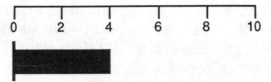

Irritation Quotient: 4

This common lack of trust on the part of cashiers results in a frustrating, time-wasting phenomenon in many stores: the price check.

Granted, when an unscrupulous or seedy-looking customer tries to snow a cashier by telling her an unmarked item is a suspiciously low price, she should by all means call for a price check. However, if a credible, nice-looking individual (like you) offers to save time by volunteering the advertised price, the cashier should accept it as gospel and get on with the punching of the keys.

Unfortunately, most of them aren't that intuitive, and they *all* possess that same attitude:

"No no, that pack o' gum isn't marked and I don't believe you when you say it's 39 cents, so I'm gonna hafta call Brenda our gum expert to come up here from waaaay back in the stockroom on her crutches to tell me the real price and then I can give you the gum which you won't be able to chew anyway because your teeth have by now fallen out in old age — Oh, hi Brenda, how much is this pack of gum? 39 cents? Okay, thanks, just wanted to make sure. Will that be all?"

Your reply: "No, I'd like each stick of gum in a separate bag!"

SHOPPERS WHO TRY TO PAY BY CREDIT CARD IN THE "CASH ONLY" LINE.

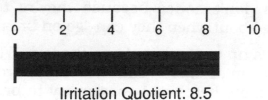

Irritation Quotient: 8.5

These intensely inconsiderate people exist not because they can't read signs but because they pledge allegiance to the "I am the Center of the Universe" theory of existence:

"Who cares what the sign says? *I* have to be first in line, and *I* pay by charge, therefore *you* will have to live with it because *I* said so!"

Here's a case where you'd love to whip out your handy-dandy tin snips and slice the offender's card into narrow plastic shards.

SHOPPERS WHO TAKE 13 OR MORE ITEMS INTO THE "12 ITEMS-OR-LESS" LINE.

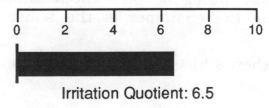

Irritation Quotient: 6.5

If somebody takes a full cart load of items into the "12 items-or-less" line, it's usually because they just plain missed the sign. That's understandable. All you do is point out their mistake and kick 'em the hell out of line.

The prime aggravators are the people who try to sneak in 13 or 15 or 20 things and pretend they miscounted. Unfortunately, although *you* can see their carts are overloaded, the never-observant cashiers don't notice because they're too busy worrying about when they can "go on break."

So, it's up to you to enforce the law. While they watch in amazement, calmly remove from their cart as many items as is necessary to bring their total down to the maximum number allowed, and drop them on the floor one at a time. Be sure to start with the eggs.

UNLOADING ALL YOUR PURCHASES ON THE COUNTER, THEN DISCOVERING THE PERSON IN FRONT OF YOU HAS TO GET HIS/HER CHECK APPROVED.

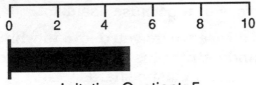

Irritation Quotient: 5

This feeling is virtually the same as the one experienced during the "price check" situation, but this time the customer is the source of the problem.

And there's just as little you can do about it, too.

ELDERLY FEMALE SHOPPERS WHO FEEL COMPELLED TO COUNT OUT EXACT CHANGE IN PENNIES.

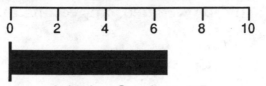

Irritation Quotient: 6.5

The combination of old ladies and coin purses is deadly.

How many times have you been in line behind a lady whose bill came to so-many-dollars and *99 cents*? You watch with dread as she proceeds to count out 99 cents in super-slow motion. And don't you know, it's not three quarters, two dimes and four pennies. No, it's four dimes, nine nickels and 14 pennies. By the time she gets to 85, the entire checkout area is counting along with her like it's New Year's Eve: "Eighty-*six* ... eighty-*seven* ..."

PEOPLE IN GROCERY CHECKOUT LINES WHO WHIP OUT THEIR COUPONS *AFTER* THEIR BILL HAS BEEN TOTALED.

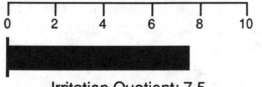

Irritation Quotient: 7.5

"Absent-minded" does not describe these individuals. "Stupid" is a little closer, but that word doesn't quite do them justice, either.

There's just no excuse for this act, and it instantly ruins the day for all the SPs behind them in the checkout line. All After-The-Fact Coupon Users should be weighed, tagged and dumped in the grocer's freezer.

SHOPPING MALLS

ENTERING A STRANGE SHOPPING MALL AND TRYING TO FIND THE DESIRED STORES ON THOSE ILLEGIBLE MALL MAPS.

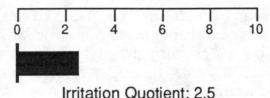

Irritation Quotient: 2.5

Whoever designed those illuminated maps you find at mall entrances obviously wanted to play games with the shoppers. The object of the game is to find on the map the store you'd like to visit, then get to it before the mall closes.

Still more panic-inducing is going to a strange mall to find a commode. Locating the word "restroom" on the map, then finding the microscopic corresponding number will surely be a challenge to your patience ... not to mention your bladder.

RUNNING INTO A MALL TO BUY ONE THING AND HAVING TO DODGE A SERIES OF HOME IMPROVEMENT BOOTH DISPLAYS.

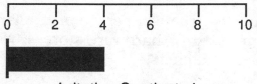

Irritation Quotient: 4

The shopping mall becomes an instant obstacle course on occasions like these. You have to steer around bodies shuffling about aimlessly on a *normal* day at the mall. Here, you have to cut through, step around or jump over sprawling home improvement displays and lawn-and-garden booths ... all to get that picture frame you wanted.

Be careful as you make your way through the mall in these situations. You might get roped into buying a prefab storage shed.

WALKING PAST A PIANO/ORGAN SHOWROOM AND HEARING SOMEONE PLAYING "THE GIRL FROM IPANEMA."

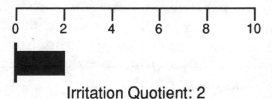

Irritation Quotient: 2

You thought this annoyance from the late sixties was dead, didn't you? Sorry, no such good fortune. The tacky practice of having an employee perform that musical dinosaur to demonstrate a keyboard is alive and well 25 years later.

These days, though, the middle-of-the-road abomination isn't being played on the Teenie Genie organ ... it's played on a booming synthesizer.

And notice, they *never* open a piano/organ showroom next to a hardware store ... where they sell axes and hatchets.

PEOPLE WHO TAKE SURVEYS IN MALLS.

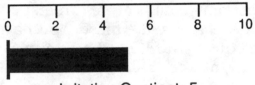

Irritation Quotient: 5

No one gets avoided like the Black Plague more than mall survey-takers. These men and women with their dark suits and clipboards look very threatening as you watch them standing there, ready to pounce on the next unsuspecting shopper.

As you approach the vicinity of the survey-taker, your best defense is to walk briskly, look at your watch and avoid all eye contact. Most of them will see you're late for something and instead accost the old lady behind you, who is struggling to carry six bags of merchandise and a giant flower pot.

PEOPLE WHO LOITER AROUND YOU IN THE "FOOD COURT" SO THEY CAN GRAB YOUR TABLE THE MOMENT YOU LEAVE.

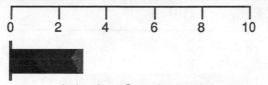

Irritation Quotient: 3

Most malls have "food courts" where you can go to have a fast-food lunch during your busy shopping day.

These areas get extremely crowded around meal times, and there isn't nearly enough seating to accommodate everybody who comes to stuff their faces.

So, if you're lucky enough to find a table, you'll notice that *Night of the Living Dead*-type people carrying loaded food trays will wander about and gravitate toward your table when it looks as though you're almost finished with your meal.

This situation makes SPs uncomfortable, feeling sort of like a rotting carcass being circled by vultures. To have some fun, finish your meal and just sit there with a zombie-like expression. See how long it takes them to move on or work up the nerve to ask if they can have your table.

145

BUMPING INTO A CASUAL ACQUAINTANCE WHO KNOWS *YOUR* NAME AND EVERYTHING ABOUT YOU, BUT WHOSE IDENTITY ESCAPES YOU.

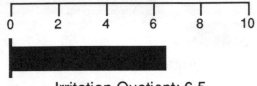

Irritation Quotient: 6.5

The last two items in this category feature the most dreaded situations to be experienced at a shopping mall. It figures they would have nothing to do with shopping.

Most Superiors try their damnedest to remain incognito at malls because there's no telling when they're going to run into someone they know, but don't care to deal with. So, if they happen to see a person they recognize but whose name isn't in their memory banks, they try to avoid him before *he* notices *them*. In those terrifying cases where a Superior hears a mysterious voice from behind calling his or her name, the blood pressure goes up, and as they turn, they hope to God it's a very good friend.

It rarely is.

Without fail, this vaguely familiar gent will rush up to you, shake your hand and inquire how you and your entire family — by individual names — are doing. All you can do is answer in generic positives and negatives and pray he doesn't wonder why you don't ask him how *his* wife and kids are, and how *his* new job is going.

The situation is even more awkward when you're with someone like your spouse because ettiquette states that you introduce them to one another. You can either let the cat out of the bag that you don't know this clown's name, or be rude and not even attempt an introduction.

Either way, you're stuck. Just act nonchalantly and if you're lucky, you'll never run into each other again in this lifetime.

BUMPING INTO SOMEONE YOU NEVER REALLY LIKED AND HAVEN'T SEEN IN YEARS AND GETTING CORNERED INTO SHARING LIFE STORIES.

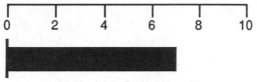

Irritation Quotient: 7

This one can be more or less aggravating than the previous item depending on how much you disliked the person you've run into.

If it's an old co-worker or schoolmate and you don't really care about him, you have to choose between time-wasting politeness and the cold shoulder.

In any case, to have an old, long-lost acquaintance ask you "what's new" is like asking you to recite the Monroe Doctrine in three minutes. It's not a practical request; it's just something to say and it puts all the pressure on you. So, you reply with something equally exciting like "Nothing" or "Oh, not much, how about you?" Then the other

147

person will say, "Nothing" and you can both be on your way to your next chance meeting ten years from now.

*　*　*

Grinning and bearing the people and the stores while shopping can be a challenge to your mental health, but it becomes even more taxing when you consider that once the shopping is finished, the real stress is only beginning ... on the way home ... on the road ... in the car ...

CATEGORY #14:
DRIVING
(On the Road and Up the Wall)

For many Superior People, driving provides the most constant bombardment of irritation of all the social situations. Rarely do you come into actual personal contact with other drivers, but nowhere are there more frustrating and galling people than on the open road.

Many Superiors return from work, school, shopping or vacations with a few more gray hairs than when they left, and not because of where they had been or what they did while they were there. Rather, it was the trip there and back that subtracted a few precious years from their lives.

Some normally easy-going individuals become obscenity-spewing monsters the second they slip behind the wheel. These people will most likely meet their end while driving — not due to a traffic accident, mind you, but because of some stress-related malady.

Here then, are the most common sources of irritation associated with the operation of an automobile.

149

PERFECTLY HEALTHY AND ABLE DRIVERS WHO PARK IN HANDICAPPED SPOTS.

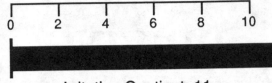

Irritation Quotient: 11

Actually, you could make a case that some of these motorists are indeed handicapped: Specifically, they must be *blind*, because they can't *see the restricted parking sign* which is as obvious as their one-digit IQs.

These vermin are among the lowest form of parasitical life on the planet. These are creatures who, every time they park in a handicapped space, commit a crime against humanity. They are inconsiderate, selfish, discourteous, unscrupulous and contemptible pieces of fungus. An apology is offered at this time to handicapped people around the world for the actions of these rodents who deliberately put themselves in front of *everyone* else. And another apology to fungus.

PEOPLE WHO LEAVE HUGE DOGS IN PARKED CARS WITH THE WINDOWS DOWN LOW ENOUGH FOR THEM TO JUMP OUT.

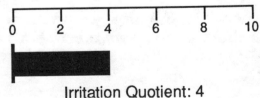

Irritation Quotient: 4

There exist Inferiors who forget that other people populate the Earth besides themselves. Idiots who go shopping and leave their Mastadon-descended canines in their cars with the windows all the way down can be classified in this category.

Imagine any normal person exiting his car, happily walking towards a store and then suddenly and involuntarily having a bowel movement at the sight and sound of a foam-mouthed dogosaurus barking and nipping at him out of a car window. Why the dog doesn't jump out to attack is never known, but that mystery only causes increased terror in this poor individual, who then blindly bolts for the store entrance and is nearly flattened by an oncoming car.

And to think all this fear and violence occurred because one dimwitted Inferior wanted to make doubly sure Poopsie had plenty of fresh air.

VEHICLES IN CROWDED PARKING LOTS THAT TAIL YOU AS YOU *WALK* TO YOUR CAR, SO THEY CAN CLAIM YOUR SPACE.

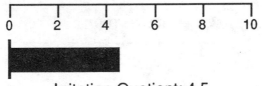

Irritation Quotient: 4.5

Ever get the feeling that Big Brother is watching you? Well, don't worry — it's really only Big Jerk *stalking* you as you head for your parking spot so he can stake his claim.

If you've got the time, one potentially hilarious remedy for the Parking Lot Skulker is to slowly wander up and down the parking aisles and see how long it takes him to realize you're only pulling his chain before he moves along.

NOT BEING ABLE TO FIND YOUR CAR IN A STRANGE OR CROWDED PARKING LOT.

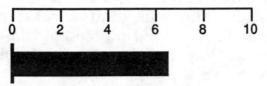

Irritation Quotient: 6.5

This is more due to your own memory lapse than anything, but it still warrants a healthy irritation. It also makes you look like an idiot as you stand alone in the lot, hands on hips, looking around baffled, trying to find your vehicle.

By the time you're convinced your car has been stolen, you suddenly remember that you had *walked* today.

PEOPLE WHO MAKE ILLEGAL U-TURNS.

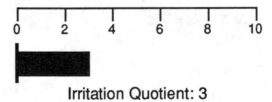

Irritation Quotient: 3

This is one of the many traffic irritations that speaks for itself. The sign says NO U-TURNS, so don't do it!

While not a serious offense, it is aggravating merely because if someone will do *that,* they may attempt other brilliant stunts like running red lights and partaking in Chinese fire drills on freeways.

MOTORISTS WHO WON'T TURN RIGHT ON RED NO MATTER WHAT.

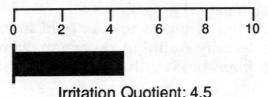

Irritation Quotient: 4.5

In most parts of the United States there is a traffic law which allows you to turn right at a red light after you've come to a complete stop.

Unfortunately, there are some folks (usually senior citizens) who believe the laws were better back in "their day" —1836— and therefore refuse to turn right on red no matter how much horn honking, finger-waving and bumper-nudging you do. They merely pretend nobody's behind them and when the light turns green, they just *might* turn, but only if they're good and ready ... you whippersnapper!

MOTORISTS WHO TAILGATE WITH THEIR BRIGHT LIGHTS ON.

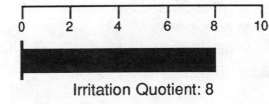

Irritation Quotient: 8

153

More of the "I am the Center of the Universe" mentality, these people want to be first and also want to see clearly at night. So on come the brights and down goes the distance between your rear fender and his front one.

A variation of this behavioral theme is the guy who wants to pass you on the highway, so he dogs right behind you and flashes his brights so you will immediately change lanes and allow him to go by. Instead of giving in to this road hog, a costly but wonderfully fulfilling deterrent would be to slam on your brakes the moment he flicks his lights.

(Yes, it would be his fault.)

DRIVERS WHO TURN LEFT WITHOUT SIGNALING.

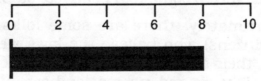

Irritation Quotient: 8

If you happen to end up behind a guy like this, you assume he'll be continuing straight ahead just like yourself — until the brake lights come on. After the Inferior has stopped, there is a split-second of mystery as to why he came to a halt in the middle of the road. Is he in need of medical attention? Is he confused? Is he out of gas? Did he misplace his accelerator?

Nope ... he's turning left, but neglected to communicate that intention to you.

The resulting irritation causes you to search for an opportunity to change lanes. It's guaranteed you'll find an opening in traffic right about the time the Inferior finally makes his turn, leaving the lane you just vacated free and clear.

Either that, or he'll turn just as the light changes to red, leaving you stopped in your tracks for another grueling two minutes.

DRIVERS WHO TURN RIGHT FROM THE CENTER LANE.

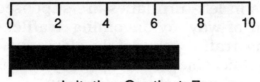

Irritation Quotient: 7

This doesn't happen all that often, but it *does* happen ... and it's an act of such radical proportions, you're not sure if you should give the person the finger or a round of applause for being so original.

Anger wins out since it was you he cut off to turn right from the center lane. You give fleeting thought to chasing this guy, but it's important that you don't because you would immediately become like him in front of witnesses.

You never want to lower yourself to Inferior Status — besides, idiots like that are probably armed.

DRIVERS IN THE CENTER LANE ACROSS FROM YOU WHO TURN LEFT IMMEDIATELY AFTER THE LIGHT TURNS GREEN.

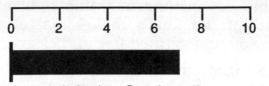

Irritation Quotient: 7

Me first! Me first!

At an intersection, when the light turns green, motorists in left-turn lanes are supposed to yield the right-of-way to oncoming traffic. Then, if oncoming traffic completely clears before their green light becomes an arrow, they can turn left at any time and be on their merry way.

It makes you wonder: is there an Inferior Person's Driving Manual we haven't heard about?

MOTORISTS WHO DON'T USE THE CONVENIENT LEFT-TURN LANE TO TURN LEFT.

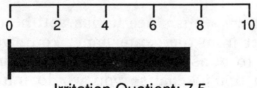

Irritation Quotient: 7.5

Many streets have a real neat middle lane used exclusively for turning left. Apparently, some folks don't know how to use it.

For drivers who get trapped behind someone who is waiting to turn left from a lane *other* than that left-turn lane, the greatest weapon is the horn. Lean on it. Even if the blaring doesn't get the pinhead to move, it'll assure your personal satisfaction.

PEOPLE WHO CUT THROUGH A CORNER GAS STATION TO AVOID WAITING AT A RED LIGHT.

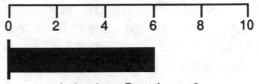

Irritation Quotient: 6

The norms and mores of society are completely ignored by the dorks and morons who can't wait at a light with everybody else.

Besides increasing the risk of mowing down someone who is innocently pumping some unleaded, this action causes Superior Spectators to lose *their* patience and cool and to flip the irritator the all-purpose bird.

DRIVERS WHO DON'T DARE ACCELERATE EVEN *ONE* MPH OVER THE SPEED LIMIT.

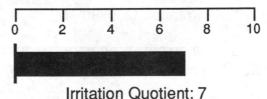

Irritation Quotient: 7

These law-abiding citizens would drive any Superior Motorist to the nearest roadside bar, especially if they are encountered in a 25 mile-per-hour zone.

Have you ever been stuck behind one of these "driverus timidus" creatures on a two-lane road? His hands are in textbook 10 o'clock/2 o'clock position and he's creeping along at exactly 25 miles an hour (or less). The nerve of some people! You get as close as possible to his rear fender, hoping you'll scare him off the road and into selling his car. (You can do this without conscience because, unlike the Guy Who Tailgates with His Brights On, you're the victim here, not the instigator.)

Alas, this trouble-making twit never sees you, and in the meantime some four-wheel-drive menace comes roaring up behind you at 55, cursing at *you* for going so slow.

TWO ACQUAINTED MOTORISTS WHO MEET ON THE ROAD AND GO 10 MILES AN HOUR WHILE THEY CONVERSE IN TRAFFIC.

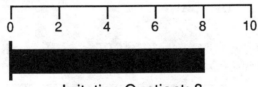

Irritation Quotient: 8

The road is a great place for people to meet friends they haven't seen in years, or so it would seem.

Exasperatingly, many times you'll be right behind a car whose driver is carrying on a chummy conversation with another motorist who is in the next lane. Since both oblivious people have to shout across a passenger seat to talk, they're forced to drive under ten miles per hour so they can hear each other.

You can't drive around 'em, and since you're a moral individual, you can't intentionally total their vehicles ... so the next best thing is to make it exceedingly difficult for *them* to carry on *their* annoying activity.

This is accomplished by rolling down all your windows, finding a heavy-metal radio station and turning it up full blast.

Hearing you, other motorists will follow suit, and eventually, this car cacophony will make the irritators wonder what the hell is going on behind them, snapping them out of their exclusive little existence.

MOTORISTS WHO RACE TO CUT YOU OFF, THEN DO 20 ONCE THEY'RE IN FRONT OF YOU.

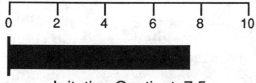

Irritation Quotient: 7.5

This type of Inferior is an alumnus of the Me First Driving School. You know the type: As you approach a side street or his driveway, he'll peel rubber to cut in front of you —as if he's terribly late — then slow down to a crawl — as if he has all day.

What was the big hurry? And now, what's the hold-up? Who is this person, Dr. Jekyll/Mr. Hyde?

DRIVERS ON AN INTERSTATE WHO, AT THE LAST SECOND, CHANGE FOUR LANES AT ONCE TO GET OFF AT AN EXIT.

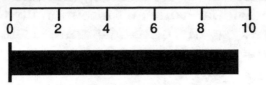

Irritation Quotient: 9.5

What, did this driver wake up from his nap and suddenly see his exit approaching?

Instead of paying for his own unobservant mistake by getting off at the *next* exit, this arrogant doofus makes everybody *else* pay for it by driving perpendicular to oncoming traffic to get off *now!*

It's moments like these that make you wish you had your own personal police flasher. After the lame-o left the highway, you'd slap your flasher on your roof and go after him in fine "unmarked police car" fashion — probably causing him to have a "trouser accident." And after you've pulled him over and made him roll down his window, you let him have a dose of shaving cream (or some other surprising substance) right in the face.

It'll take him days to recover from the psychological damage alone.

Ah, if only life worked that way....

WORKING HARD TO GET INTO ANOTHER LANE WHICH YOU THEN DISCOVER IS CLOSED 500 FEET AHEAD.

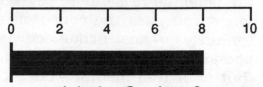

Irritation Quotient: 8

Here's a classic rush hour vexation which truly makes you want to drive up somebody's tailpipe.

You're coming home from a rough work day and you are preparing to perform the same driving ritual you do every day. You use the same route, the same freeway exit, even the exact same lanes in the exact same locations every single time.

At one crucial merge area, it's necessary to get in the right lane so as to split off to a different highway, otherwise you'll end up 400 miles from home with no hope of making it back in time for dinner. So, every day at about the same time, you reach the split, engage your directional indicator and fight like hell to get over before you run out of road.

The good news is, like every other day, you successfully make the move. The bad news is, for some reason, today your lane is closed 500 feet ahead due to construction, and you can make out orange rubber cones up ahead which force all the traffic that had been in the lane to *begin* with (besides you) back into the congested lane you just *left*. Then you'll have to perform the whole lane-changing process again, all without having that breakdown which would feel so good about now.

161

This same irritation can be caused by a stalled car or an accident, but a lane closed for construction has the potential to be more severely irritating, like when you pass the coned-off area and witness absolutely *no* construction activity at all — maybe some guys in hard-hats standing around pointing, but no actual men at work. It's almost like some bored city employees with a malicious sense of humor planted the cones just to watch drivers gnashing their teeth as they pass.

In addition to all this mental anguish, it's almost certain the lane closed due to alleged construction will be totally overlooked on the radio traffic reports — that is, until you've passed through it.

RUBBERNECKERS WHO SLOW FREEWAY TRAFFIC DOWN, EVEN THOUGH THE ACCIDENT THEY'RE WATCHING IS ON THE *OTHER SIDE* OF THE MEDIAN.

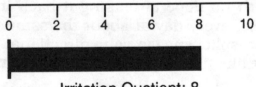

Irritation Quotient: 8

Incredibly frustrating, isn't it? Especially during rush hour. Nothing attracts attention like blood and guts, so even though an accident is on the other side of the concrete dividing wall, people with necks of elastic would rather create traffic problems to see some viscera than keep things running up to speed by minding their own business.

You never see anything anyway, except for maybe some cops with their hands on their hips and the occasional overturned car.

HAVING THE LIGHT TURN GREEN THE MILLISECOND YOUR CAR COMES TO A COMPLETE STOP.

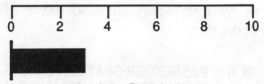

Irritation Quotient: 3

This happens so often, it's almost a subconscious game now. You can make any red light turn green whenever you want simply by deciding at what point to come to a *complete* stop. Traffic lights apparently have a "brake sensor" built into them which turns the light green the second you are forced to start accelerating all over again.

PEOPLE WHO HONK THEIR HORNS ONE SECOND OR LESS AFTER THE LIGHT HAS TURNED GREEN.

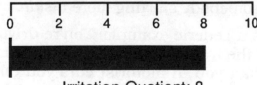

Irritation Quotient: 8

Here's more of the unjustifiably impatient "Center of the Universe" train of thought.

In this case, the enemy is just mad because he's not first in line, so to get even with the driver who *is*, he poises his fist over the horn and pounds on it the moment the green light appears.

Dirty looks and mumbled expletives inevitably ensue, but the only effective response to this horn-blasting cretin is to stay put ... until the person behind *him* starts honking, giving him a taste of his own medicine. Or, if he's the only one behind you, pretend your car has stalled out — when the light turns yellow, start up and drive off, leaving him at a red light.

SOMEONE IN THE PASSENGER SEAT DISPLAYING ANGER AT OTHER DRIVERS BY HONKING *YOUR* HORN FOR YOU.

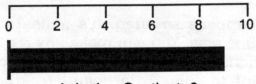

Irritation Quotient: 9

This habit of passengers riding in *your own* car is greatly vexing because they're sticking their nose (and hand) into something that's none of their business. You've got enough problems worrying about traffic irritations *outside* your car without somebody starting more *inside*.

Here's a generic example: You're driving with a friend in the front passenger seat who is more excitable than you. A motorist cuts you off and you do your customary hand gestures and cursing. Your friend, however, gets hostile, leans over to your side of the car and pounds on the horn.

Here's how to react: You immediately slam on the brakes, furiously throw his limb away from the steering wheel and shout at him to get out of the car. Once he's vacated your vehicle in amazement, speed away and drive around the block before picking him up again. His temporary belief that you really did abandon him will convince him never to invade your personal space again. That, or he'll think your nuts.

Either way, it'll cause him to mind his own business next time.

DRIVERS WHO WON'T GO OVER RAILROAD TRACKS, EVEN THOUGH THE TRAIN HAS PLAINLY STOPPED A HALF-MILE AWAY.

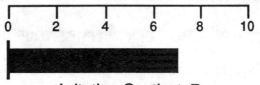

Irritation Quotient: 7

Sorry to say, but these offenders are usually senior citizens who perceive objects moving faster than they really are.

These folks cause unnecessary traffic jams (and emotional stress) that they are totally oblivious to since they're so busy watching the distant train ... which by now is backing up in the *other* direction.

MOTORISTS WHO PASS FREEWAY TRAFFIC ON THE SHOULDER SO THEY CAN SNEAK INTO YOUR LANE FURTHER AHEAD.

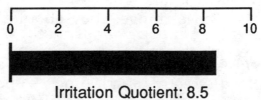

Irritation Quotient: 8.5

Still more of the Me First group of Inferior Drivers who cannot wait in traffic with all of those "common peons."

One can fantasize about a perfect world where those "common peons" gain their collective revenge on this person: They'll form a strategically-altered traffic jam which leads to the edge of a cliff, and watch with glee as the irritator goes to claim his rightful place at the front of the line ... that is, the bottom of the ravine.

MOTORISTS WHO DON'T ACKNOWLEDGE YOUR COURTEOUS ACT.

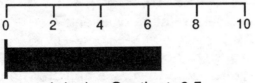

Irritation Quotient: 6.5

On a good day, you meet some of the nicest people on the road ... charitable folks who let you in front of them when you're trying to merge into their lane ... generous souls who make sure not to block a driveway you're trying to turn left into.

Sound familiar? Sure it does, because you as a Superior Person practice those same traffic courtesies. In fact, you shouldn't even have to think about doing those things; they should be reflex actions.

The real fact is, many of your kind acts as a motorist lead directly to irritation — specifically, when the driver you were kind to offers no sign of thanks whatsoever. No nod, no smile, no wave in your direction, no nothing. The ingrate just barrels on through while you notice his auto is being held together with coat hangers and duct tape.

And as you drive off, you see him going out of his way to wave at the woman with the short-shorts walking down the street. The man does have priorities, after all.

WAITING TO TURN WHILE A PEDESTRIAN CROSSES THE STREET IN SUPER-SLOW-MOTION.

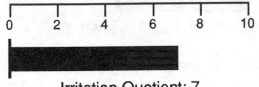

Irritation Quotient: 7

Most courteous Superior Pedestrians will break into a trot or an accelerated walking pace when they see a car waiting for them to clear the crosswalk so it can turn.

These considerate walkers are nowhere to be found, however, when it's *your* car that's doing the turning. No, these pedestrians pretend you don't exist while they stretch their right to occupy the crosswalk to the absolute limit, instead of getting some quality exercise by stepping a little faster.

School kids are even worse. The minute they notice you waiting to turn, they slow down to a shuffle, almost daring you to hit them, while impudently keeping eye contact with you all the way.

If you've got the guts, and if it's a nice neighborhood, put your car in park, put a crazed look on your face, shoot out of your car and chase after the lead-footed loser. Nine times out of ten they'll show you how fast they really *can* run.

It's that tenth time you've gotta watch out for, though.

HAVING YOUR CAR MALFUNCTION WHEN YOUR FATHER IS AROUND.

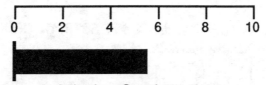

Irritation Quotient: 5.5

Anyone who ever had a dad knows the feelings of frustration and inferiority which come over you when your car breaks down or starts to leak when Pop is around.

It's then that the classic fatherly lines are spoken:

"You really ought to take better care of your car, Son."

"When was the last time you had this looked at?"

"You think this is a toy?"

Little does he know that due to your long instilled father/car paranoia, you've *been* checking the fluids twice a day, and the car's been in the *shop* more than it's been in your garage!

There's really only one solution: next time you go visit your father, ride a bike.

MOTORISTS WHO WANT EVERYONE TO KNOW THEY NEED A NEW MUFFLER.

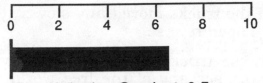

Irritation Quotient: 6.5

The sound of a defective muffler is a status symbol for most teenage burnouts and motorheads (and those who ceased maturing in the teenage years). These delinquents love to proclaim to everyone on the road and in their homes that it's cool to have no muffler by taking off jack rabbit-style from lights, tearing up and down residential streets and constantly goosing the engine in their driveways.

There is little you can do about these noise polluters — unless you know where they live. In this case, with your finger, write an appropriate message on the trunk of their dust-ridden bomb ... something like "I dare you to arrest me, Pig!"

GETTING STUCK BEHIND A SEMI, CEMENT MIXER OR CAR-CARRIER ON A TWO LANE ROAD, GOING UPHILL.

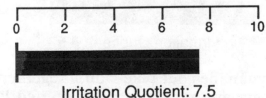

Irritation Quotient: 7.5

This situation produces one of the most helpless road irritations one can experience for the following reasons:

1) If the trucks moved any slower, they'd be going in reverse.

2) These trucks are so big and wide, you can't see any of the free world that's in front of them.

All you can see are 23 different out-of-state license plates or a red sign that announces, "How am I driving? Call ..."

The worst trucks to follow on an incline are cement mixers and loaded car-carriers. To get behind one of these vehicles is to transform an exasperating driving experience into a life-threatening one.

The morning headline would be humorous, though: "Motorist crushed by ten falling cars" or "Driver drowns in wet cement."

PEOPLE WHO RIDE BICYCLES AND MOPEDS ON TWO-LANE ROADS.

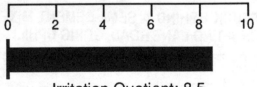

Irritation Quotient: 8.5

Happy families out bike-riding together on two-lane streets are asking to get flattened like Fruit Roll-ups for their self-centered use of these roads. It's difficult to pass them even in light traffic because they usually pedal four or five across so they can smile at each other.

When you finally do pass them, yell, "That's what they make bike paths for, idiots!"

Mopeds are even worse, because they have been allowed to travel pretty much anywhere. A limp-wristed version of the motorcycle, the moped constantly vexes the drivers of *real* motor vehicles capable of moving more than ten miles per hour.

It's about time to boycott the toy companies that make these contraptions.

DRIVING ON A SIDE STREET AND PASSING AN ONCOMING CAR PRECISELY AT THE POINT WHERE A *THIRD* CAR IS PARKED.

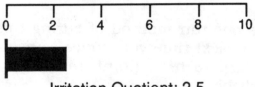

Irritation Quotient: 2.5

It's interesting to analyze why this phenomenon causes irritation:

1) It doesn't *have* to happen that way, but nine times out of ten it does.

2) Because it does, you are forced to momentarily squeeze three cars across a narrow two-lane road, risking fender removal and paint job scrapes.

DRIVERS WHO FEEL COMPELLED TO LOOK AT EVERYONE THEY PULL UP ALONGSIDE.

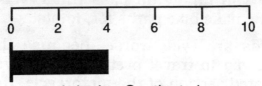

Irritation Quotient: 4

Every person in a car is in his or her own space. An Inferior who pulls up alongside a car and for no reason looks into a stranger's window is infringing on your personal space. Maybe this violator is bored or just curious about the snazzy interior of his neighbor's auto, but Superiors hate it when someone beside them at a light is staring at them.

Here's one fun method of curing this voyeuristic habit: Next time you notice someone looking at you, turn to him, point and begin laughing uncontrollably.

It's almost guaranteed he'll turn away and pretend he never saw you.

RENTAL CAR AGENTS WHO STRONGLY "URGE" YOU TO BUY INSURANCE.

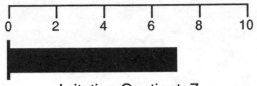

Irritation Quotient: 7

High-pressure selling at its worst can be experienced when renting a car at an airport. Those clerks are boldly determined to scare you into buying insurance at exorbitant rates ... so you can have "peace of mind" while you're driving your temporary vehicle.

What they never tell you is that your regular auto insurance (which you're shelling out exorbitant rates for in the first place) covers anything you do in a rental car.

So, when these rental company schleps start to hassle you despite the fact that you've politely refused their insurance offer four times, feel free to get rude. They get paid to give *and* take abuse.

And for an added touch — lay rubber as you leave their lot.

* * *

Doesn't it seem like you spend a good portion of your life inside your car ... in traffic or waiting in a parking lot? Don't you think the simple act of driving an automobile is often as much fun as the prospect of having a root canal done?

Well, of course! But while cars may indeed be hazardous to your health, there is so much other "stuff" occurring in an SP's general existence, his/her personal Superiority is put to the test every waking minute of every day, even without the aid of four wheels and an engine...

CATEGORY #15:
GENERAL EXISTENCE
(Bunglers in the Jungle)

Life's been good to you so far. The previous fourteen chapters have introduced you to irritations which accompany specific social situations or certain unavoidable aspects of day-to-day existence.

When you're involved in life situations like working or watching television or driving or going to an amusement park, you expect certain things to happen — both positive and negative. So, while the items discussed up to this point are indeed irritating, they are not totally, *completely* unwarranted. They go with their territory, as it were.

This final chapter will delve into those nerve-frayers which present themselves utterly "out of the blue." The only things they have in common are:

1) They may accost you at any time and/or place.

2) They involve—without exception—human beings. People: Their undesirable

176

habits and patience-eroding idiosynch-rasies.

The tainters of general existence are as follows:

PEOPLE WHO USE THE WORD "PARTY" AS A VERB.

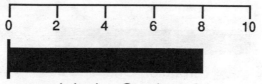

Irritation Quotient: 8

It is true that many, *many* people use that word as a verb these days:

"Hey man, wanna party?"

"She's partied out."

"We were partying all weekend long."

"Party on, Dude!"

While the verbal usage of "party" now seems unavoidable, it still induces agitation when spoken by someone who looks and acts like he or she believes that's the only usage of the word. It's that man or woman who lives to "party."

"Can't wait 'til Friday so I can party, party, party!" (Translation: "My life is so miserably dull, I can't wait until I can get wasted, puke repeatedly and not remember anything about the entire weekend.")

This annoyance stems from the fact that "partiers" generally reject reality, so they must create their own version of it. So party animals, if

177

you wanna get faced, go ahead — but stay outta Superior People's faces. They don't wanna hear about it.

PEOPLE WHOSE FAVORITE SPORT IS DRINKING.

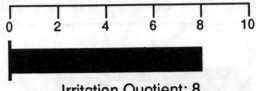

Irritation Quotient: 8

These folks are similar to the "partiers" in the previous item, but in this instance the drinkers have completely adopted their activity as a way of life.

These major league drinkers go to bars every night, just like the characters of Norm and Cliff on *Cheers*. Don't these people have homes? Jobs? Lives?

The answer to all three of those questions is probably "No," which is sad. However, in another way it makes you steamed because as a Superior Person, *you* work hard, *you* care about your life and the lives in it, *you* make serious attempts to improve your existence.

Why can't they??

PEOPLE WHO DEVOUR ALCOHOL, BUT STAUNCHLY CLAIM THEY "DON'T DRINK."

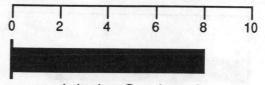

Irritation Quotient: 8

This type of Inferior desperately wants to be a Superior, but ultimately cannot and will not be. A tell-tale characteristic of this person is drinking, but actually believing he *doesn't*.

To this so-called *Non-Drinker*, "I don't drink" means, "Well, I do drink beer, but it doesn't really affect me that much and I only get really drunk twice a month and on special occasions, but I know when to stop, so I'm no alcoholic."

When one of these phonies claim "I don't drink!" substitute a "th" for the "dr" in "drink" and you get a more accurate autobiographical revelation.

PEOPLE WHO DON'T LOOK AT YOU WHILE YOU CONVERSE WITH THEM.

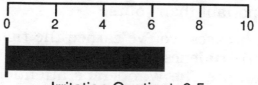

Irritation Quotient: 6.5

179

PEOPLE WHO INTERRUPT YOU WHEN YOU'RE TALKING TO SOMEONE ELSE.

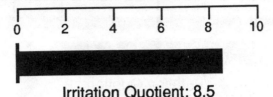

Irritation Quotient: 8.5

Both of these related items cause much wailing and gnashing of dental work, because both violate a simple, easy-to-adhere-to law: Courtesy.

Superiors are not generally known as people who run off at the mouth. They choose their words carefully and speak when they believe their words will be listened to and appreciated.

So, a person who doesn't keep eye contact with you at least part of the time you're talking ("The Wanderer") either really *isn't* interested in what you're saying, or is thoughtlessly devoting his attention to something *more* fascinating. Somebody who interrupts you while you're conversing with someone else ("The Wedge") is even more rude, because he thinks *his* topic or point of view or maybe even his entire existence on this planet is more important than yours.

In both cases, you've earned the right to exercise a little rudeness right back at the insolence. When you see The Wanderer's attention waning, grab his face and begin speaking slowly, e-nun-ci-a-ting clear-ly and loud-ly. As for The Wedge, the minute he interrupts, clamp your hand over his mouth and continue your conversation as though nothing happened. Both ways, your point will be made, and the Law of Courtesy will be enforced.

PEOPLE OTHER THAN CLOSE LOVED ONES WHO MAKE PHONY "KISSY-FACE" WHEN GREETING YOU.

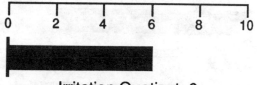

Irritation Quotient: 6

Like most other humans, Superiors enjoy kissing. Superior spouses and lovers do it all the time. With relatives, it's a normal sign of love and affection.

Contrarily, when they see a twice-removed aunt they run into every eleven years, they genuinely have no desire to smooch them. This is due largely to the fact that there never was an intimate relationship there, so a kiss isn't necessary. When they wrap their limbs around you and start to pucker up, instead of being a sign of affection, the kiss becomes a sign of phoniness.

It's the same when Sammy Davis, Jr. kisses Jerry Lewis on the Labor Day Telethon. All that mock sincerity and stroking just isn't convincing. It's as if they're saying, "Look everybody! We like each other! Please like us for liking each other!"

PEOPLE WHO COUGH OR SNEEZE INTO THEIR PALM IMMEDIATELY BEFORE SHAKING HANDS WITH YOU.

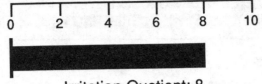

Irritation Quotient: 8

It's quite common for someone to absent-mindedly spew something into his palm just as you are extending your hand to him. At this point, you must make a split-second decision: Be rude or slimy. The more desirable choice is, of course, the former. Withdrawing your hand also makes the Inferior Person cognizant of the gross thing he just did.

What he needs is a special *Hand Condom* so he can practice *safe handshakes*.

ANYONE BESIDES THE PEOPLE YOU LIVE WITH COMING TO YOUR RESIDENCE UNANNOUNCED.

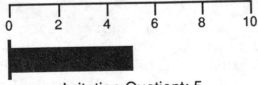

Irritation Quotient: 5

A favorite pastime of relatives, "dropping by" unannounced only succeeds in screwing up the timetable of the typical, super-organized Superior Person. When he or she hears a knock on the door or a musical voice through the window calling, "Anybody hoooome?", an SP will register a look of horror and attempt to nonverbally communicate to the intruders that they are not wanted here at this time.

It doesn't work, of course, and the Superior is forced to spend time with them — physically, at least, since the mind will be occupied with figuring out how to get back on schedule.

Don't offer your visitors any food or beverage, look at your watch a lot and pace back and forth continuously. Somewhere along the way they should get the message and get lost.

PEOPLE WHO ARE ALWAYS LATE.

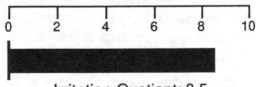

Irritation Quotient: 8.5

Because of their concern for organization, Superiors hate to be late for anything. That's why they are so intolerant of someone else who is repeatedly late for *them.*

A forever-tardy Inferior is the kind of happy-go-lucky floater who interprets "be there at eight o'clock" as "set your *alarm* for eight o'clock." Time-pieces are not big parts of an always-late person's existence and he doesn't really care if he's late or early anyway. He'll get there when he gets there.

If you happen to work for a chronically-late person, all you can do is look a little miffed. If a late person works for you, in one respect you're lucky: you can fire him.

In a non-work situation, "a taste of their own" is sometimes the best medicine. When the chronic late person is expecting *you*, turn up way beyond the appointed time — like the next day.

PEOPLE WHO DON'T CALL TO *SAY* THEY ARE GOING TO BE LATE.

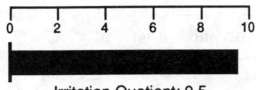

Irritation Quotient: 9.5

While it is maddening to deal with a "flotsam and jetsam person" who is forever tardy, at least he becomes predictable after a while, and you can then adapt and work around him.

The person who you can count on to be late is not as maddening as the person who is occasionally late and fails to call to say so. Even more angering is when he doesn't offer any explanation for his tardiness *once he does arrive*. It's as if he just assumed you would wait for him — that thoroughly contemptible "I am the Center of the Universe" mentality rears its ugly head again, causing you to put your life into cryogenic freeze while you wait for this moron to show up.

Service-oriented people are often guilty of this discourtesy (i.e. cement contractors, builders, landscapers). They believe your life depends on *them*, rather than the other way around, so they think they can show up ... or *not* show up ... at the appointed time, depending on the mood they're in. Then, when they offer no excuse for their lack of responsibility, they wonder why *you're* so upset!

Yet these same people are on the phone to remind you the very *minute* your bill becomes overdue.

PEOPLE WHO DEMAND A WINDOW SEAT ON AN AIRPLANE, THEN KEEP THE SHADE DOWN THE ENTIRE FLIGHT.

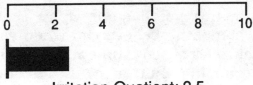

Irritation Quotient: 2.5

Why don't these people just buy their own private jet? They obviously think they own the ones they fly economy on, since they monopolize a window seat, then leave the shade down while they read or take a nap. This self-centered act leaves you with a panoramic view up the guy's nostrils, as opposed to any sort of breathtaking scenery.

Ah, just as well. You'd probably see some strange gremlin-like creature on the wing of the plane sabotaging one of the engines.

PEOPLE WHO REPEATEDLY ASK YOU IF YOU'RE *SURE* YOU DON'T WANT SOMETHING TO EAT OR DRINK.

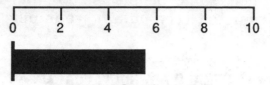

Irritation Quotient: 5.5

Occasionally, you'll come upon that host or hostess who doesn't believe you when you politely refuse their offer of refreshment. Here's how some typical annoying banter would occur in this situation:

"Would you like something to drink?"

"Oh, no thanks. I'm fine."

"You sure? How 'bout some pop? I've got Pepsi."

"Thanks, really. Maybe a little later."

"Come on, you look thirsty. How 'bout some orange juice?"

"Ummm, I *just* had something a few minutes before I got here. Thank you anyway."

"Here, I'll pour you some iced tea..."

(Grabbing collar) "Damn it! I <u>said</u> Noooooo!"

Then they label *you* belligerent and rude.

By the second refusal, the pushy irritator should have buttoned his or her overly-hospitable lip, but in the quest to be the Perfect Host, he or she is willing to drive the guest insane.

PEOPLE WHO, WHEN YOU ASK THEM WHAT THEY JUST MUMBLED, SAY, "NOTHING."

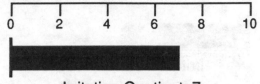

Irritation Quotient: 7

Individuals who desperately want to make a caustic comment, but who don't have the guts to say it aloud, are most often guilty of this irritating crime.

Someone will set himself up for a wisecrack and this person will be heard saying something like, "Yeah, mmmblmmblllllng." You then ask, "What was that?" To which the mumbler will reply:

"Oh, nothing."

Superior temperatures then rise, because what was mumbled was not "nothing," but indeed "something," which now has to be pried from the larynx of this wimp!

"CUTE" COUPLES WHO DRESS ALIKE.

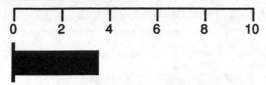

Irritation Quotient: 3.5

No, not parents who dress their twin babies up the exact same way ... although that practice *can* cause big identity problems for the kids later in life.

What this item calls attention to is the sickly-sweet, cute, yuppie-type man and woman who wear the same color and style shirts and slacks in public places. Or maybe cutesy T-shirts that read, "I'm hers" and "I'm his."

Gaaaggg! Not only does individuality go right out the window, but saccharine obnoxiousness takes its place, and the whole idea coupled with their syrupy smiling faces makes you wanna run up to them and smack them senseless.

But don't do that. Just roll your eyes, make faces and laugh to yourself.

PEOPLE WHO FORCE THEIR HEAVY METAL OR DANCE-MUSIC TASTES ON YOU IN PUBLIC BY BLARING THEIR BOOM-BOX.

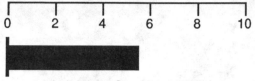

Irritation Quotient: 5.5

Teenagers who don't like taking out the garbage or lifting heavy equipment at their bonehead jobs will curiously go to the trouble of toting around a bulky boom-box just so they can blast their tedious brand of thumpa-thumpa or metal-head tunes in public places, causing motorists to drive into ditches and pedestrians to double over in pain while clutching their bleeding ears.

A miniature, easy-to-conceal squirt gun is the best remedy here. A strategic jet of water to the area of the "PLAY" button will usually seep inside and cause a short-circuit. Excellent aim is required in order to make an *undetected* "hit". "Undetected" is highly stressed. When you consider the caliber of sub-human that usually carries a boom box, the last thing you want is to make him mad at *you.*

PEOPLE WHO EXIT A PUBLIC BUILDING AND PROCEED TO BLOCK THE DOORWAY WHILE THEY DECIDE WHICH DIRECTION TO WALK.

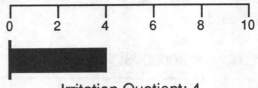

Irritation Quotient: 4

This is one of those "World Stops for Me" habits which not only cause bottlenecks in doorways but also aneurysms in the protruding neck veins of Superiors caught in those doorways.

When you are victimized here, peer over the irritant's shoulder and ask him if he has heard the Word of God today. He'll move.

PEOPLE WHO DON'T WATCH WHERE THEY'RE WALKING.

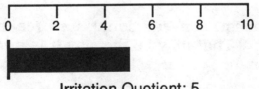

Irritation Quotient: 5

There are times when you'd swear a breed of genetically-altered human is loose in your neighborhood that has a head permanently turned at a 90-degree angle.

This breed walks like every other human, but can't see where it's going, and so is always bumping into people and things.

When you notice one unwittingly approaching you, evasive action is useless. You can dodge and weave but his built-in homing device will cause him to parallel your every maneuver — until you inevitably collide.

PEOPLE WHO ASK RIDICULOUSLY OBVIOUS QUESTIONS.

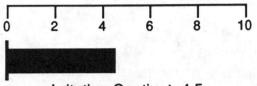

Irritation Quotient: 4.5

You know these jokers. They ask questions like "Oh, is this office being used?" to a roomful of people sitting around a conference table.

One of the all-time great obvious interrogatives is directed at men: "Hey, are you growing a beard?"

An honest, conversational, ice-breaking question, right? That may be the way it is intended by the asker, but to the askee it sounds exceedingly stupid.

Analyze it. The reason someone asks this question in the first place is because there is detectable growth on the guy's face, which means whether he wanted to or not, he's growing a beard! Therefore the question is superfluous and merits a sarcastic response like, "No, I bought this at a stubble store."

PEOPLE WHO, WHEN BUYING BIRTHDAY GIFTS FOR FRIENDS, DELIBERATELY IMPOSE THEIR OWN TASTES ON THEM.

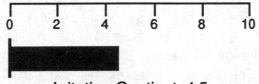

Irritation Quotient: 4.5

How selfish! If it's your birthday and a friend who collects ceramic skulls gives *you* a ceramic skull as a present, how are you supposed to react? "Gee ... thanks ... it'll look great as a centerpiece on our dinner table."

What's worse are the days and weeks after the gift has been given, because you know your pal is going to want to *see* that wonderful piece of art displayed on your fireplace mantle or some other place of honor.

In reality, when all is unwrapped and done, your friend bought the gift for his own materialistic ends. He doesn't really care if you wanted it or not! *He* thinks it's cool or impressive, and that's all that really matters to him.

You as the recipient, on the other hand, should waste no time in taking the completely useless and/or tasteless item back from whence it came for a full refund. Then you can use the money for something you really want.

And to think, all that time-wasting inconvenience and awkward trying-to-look-pleased would have been saved if your crony had simply thought about *your* tastes, instead of imposing *his* tastes on you.

The thing to do if this gift-giving pattern develops with one of your acquaintances, is to keep a count of how often you get an off-the-wall present. Then, begin reciprocating by giving *him* velvet renderings of Clint Eastwood, along with other "gifty" collectibles available in the parking lot of your corner service station.

RELATIVES AND FRIENDS WHO BUY YOU THINGS FOR ULTERIOR REASONS.

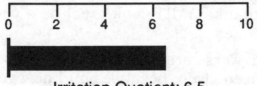

Irritation Quotient: 6.5

"Can't buy me love."

Oh yeah? Try telling that to acquaintances and kin who are always buying things for functionally self-sufficient people (a.k.a. Superiors) — with the excuse, "just because I felt like it."

But the fact is, there is *always* a reason behind their alleged "nice gestures." Now, this is not the guy who buys his date flowers or some trinket. It's not the wife who gives the husband a present for no particular occasion. No. There are legitimate reasons for *those* gift-giving occasions. Reasons like genuine affection and love.

Who it *is*, is Aunt Ethel who buys you a completely unwarranted Belgian Waffle at the family picnic because "you look hungry" — but really it's because she wants to publicly demonstrate how "generous" she is. And it's pal Murray who presents you with "a small token" right before informing you he's separated from his wife and looking for a place to live.

These are either seriously insecure individuals or worse yet, users and abusers. The end result of these head games is always *guilt,* whether it's intentionally inflicted or not. So, whenever possible, refuse their gifts — unless by complete accident it's something you can really use.

PEOPLE WHO HABITUALLY MANGLE THE PRONUNCIATIONS OF COMMON ENGLISH WORDS.

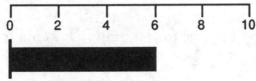

Irritation Quotient: 6

There are people in America — many possessing above-average intelligence — who, through repeated usage, misguided teaching or just plain laziness, make mincemeat out of everyday English words.

These people are Word Butchers, and they will even *read* correctly-spelled words in their own customized incorrect style. When they commit gross oral offenses like these, eyebrows raise and any credibility they have established up to that point begins to rapidly decrease.

Here are a few fingernail-bending examples of words commonly dismembered by Inferior People:

Correct Pronunciation	Inferior Pronunciation
ESCAPE	EXCAPE

(i.e. "The policeman let his prisoner *excape.*")

ESPECIALLY	EXPECIALLY

(i.e. "I would *expecially* like to take you to dinner.")

NUCLEAR	NOOKYALER

(i.e. "I work for the *Nookyaler* Regulatory Commission.")

YOU	YOUZ

(i.e. "*Youz* guys better get an education.")

PROBABLY	PROBLY

(i.e. "You'll *probly* never be an English teacher.")

BIRTHDAY	BURFDAY

(i.e. "Happy *burfday* to you, happy *burfday* to you.")

GRANTED	GRANITE

(i.e. "He took the whole thing for *granite.*")

TREK	TRACK

(i.e. "Hey, look! It's Doctor Spock from 'Star *Track!*'")

TRACK	TRACT

(i.e. "Let's keep *tract* of the score.")

INTENTS AND	INTENSIVE

(i.e. "For all *intensive* purposes, I am a moron.")

These ten examples merely scratch the surface of a very patience-trying problem. As a rule of thumb, Word Butchers should be severely corrected at every oral offense perpetrated. Make them learn they won't get away with their plan to undermine the foundation of the Americanese language.

MEN WHO REFER TO THEIR GIRLFRIENDS OR WIVES AS "THE WIFE."

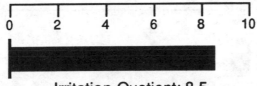

Irritation Quotient: 8.5

Women, whether or not you're present when this happens, you are the victims of severe disrespect every time your men refer to you as "the wife," "the old lady" or "the little woman." Men who truly hold their women dear simply don't even *think* of identifying them in that condescending fashion.

Interestingly, the most insulting word in these monikers is "the." *"The* wife" instead of *"My* wife" tells you you're no more than a piece of dented furniture to him; an object he keeps at home because he's got nothing better to do with you. It communicates to others that he feels he is trapped in your relationship instead of being there voluntarily.

Divorce would be a good solution for both of you here, but there's no need to rush things. Begin your retribution slowly by referring to him as "the husband" or "the old man." Then move on to "the jerk" and "the pinhead," and if he's still calling you "the wife," go ahead and start the proceedings.

PEOPLE WHO PUT TACKY PROTECTIVE COVERS ON THEIR FURNITURE.

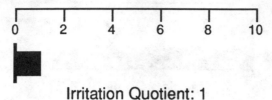

Irritation Quotient: 1

Haven't they ever heard of Scotch-Guard?

Folks who buy new couches, easy chairs and rockers, then camouflage them with bad plastic covers or drop cloth-like sheets are at once irritating and hilarious.

Furniture is made to *sit on,* isn't it?

These people also tend to put separate throw-rugs or plastic runners on their virgin carpeting. Consequently, their living rooms resemble museum exhibits more than *living* rooms. All they need is a velvet rope-and-pole set-up, then they can charge their guests admission to see their perfectly-preserved furniture while they brag that their house is an historical landmark.

SEEING THE CITY SNOW PLOW COMING DOWN YOUR STREET RIGHT AFTER YOU'VE SHOVELED YOUR DRIVEWAY APRON.

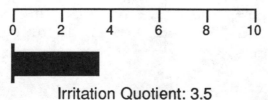

Irritation Quotient: 3.5

This is a traditional wintertime irritation similar to watching it start to rain after you've had your car washed. All you snow-belt Superiors know what the street plow does to your driveway entrance as it whisks by. For the uninitiated, it dumps about three tons of hard ice and snow in the apron so you can't pull your car out. Having to struggle with that weight is bad enough, but it's even more peeving when you've already shoveled the area once or twice that same day.

Before too long you'll decide it's time to go out and buy that newfangled snowblower — as soon as you can get your car out of the driveway, of course.

PEOPLE WHO CLIP THEIR FINGERNAILS IN PUBLIC.

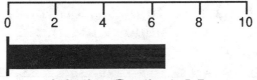

Irritation Quotient: 6.5

Chronic fingernail-clippers are people who ought to take up residence in a zoo — specifically in the monkey cage, where public grooming is accepted behavior.

Besides the gross physical residue this awful habit leaves behind, that grating *tick* ... *tick* ... *tick* sound the clippers make is enough to convince *you* to clip somebody.

If it's any help, take solace that usually these people have the decency to wait, at least until they're in the privacy of their homes, to bite their toenails.

PEOPLE WHO DON'T FLUSH THE TOILET AFTER THEY'RE DONE.

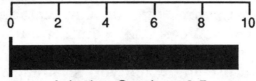

Irritation Quotient: 9.5

This amazing latrine behavior frequently occurs in public restrooms so the identity of the excretor can remain a secret.

These backwoods individuals possess old privy habits which have refused to die, even in a civilized setting. Obviously some drastic behavioral modifications need to occur, but until that next step in human evolution is taken, it's up to you, the Superior Person, to avoid public restrooms whenever possible. Because, you see, there is no way to get revenge on the anonymous primate who preceded you, unless you care to employ the rarely used science of dusting for buttprints.

STRANGERS WHO FEEL CONSTRAINED TO INITIATE A CONVERSATION BY SPOUTING SOME OPINIONATED COMMENT.

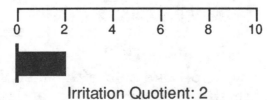

Irritation Quotient: 2

200

Some people who suddenly start talking to you like they've known you all their lives suffer from Hyper-Bitter-Loneliness. Their condition is sad, but you really can't help them, so don't even try. You'll have a hard enough time putting up with the nerve-wracking effects the sickness has on *you*.

Hypothetical example: You're waiting for a bus, minding your own affairs, when suddenly the coot next to you will turn and spontaneously blurt, "These damn kids today are all screwed up!"

At this point, most SPs will simply ignore the person, or perhaps even find another, more comfortable bus stop further down the street. However, if you're into retaliation and reverse irritation, start talking back at the stranger about the benefits of heavy-metal music, controlled substances and youth gangs, and see if you can't make him come after you with his umbrella.

Before you provoke him, though, make sure he's not the replacement bus driver.

ELDERLY RELATIVES WHO TREAT YOU LIKE YOU STOPPED AGING AT TWELVE.

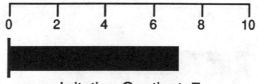

Irritation Quotient: 7

When your elderly relatives' memories first stopped functioning, you were about twelve years old. So, while they still complain about their *own* aging process, in their eyes *you're* still twelve.

They still have to plant that saliva-ridden smooch on your cheek, talk to you in that sing-songy voice and, worst of all, call you by your embarrassing childhood nickname.

Like, for example, "Bucky."

Both Bucky's and his father's name was Bob, so someone had the bright idea to call the boy "Bucky" so they *both* wouldn't answer when his mother called for "Bob." As is usually the case, though, long-range effects of childhood traumas aren't considered, and Bob the younger grows up to hate that nickname. (Obviously, the father hated it, too. That's why the *kid* got stuck with it.)

Eventually it is all but forgotten, but as the years go by, the former Bucky is always reminded of the detested name at family get-togethers.

Indeed, Bucky/Bob has just cause to be irritated, but it could have been worse. His parents *could* have called him "Binky" or "Slugger."

ELDERLY PEOPLE WHO TALK WITH GREAT ENTHUSIASM ABOUT PHYSICAL AILMENTS AND LINGERING PAIN.

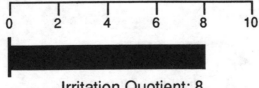

Irritation Quotient: 8

Thelma's spleen operation and Cecil's prostate surgery are always hot topics of conversation at the dinner table when there are two or more senior citizens present.

When the golden-agers start their medical version of "Can You Top This?" you might as well forget about smooth digestion for the rest of the evening. They love to talk up their goiter problems or how Uncle Arnie's colon ripped away from his small intestine or — still one of the best gross-outs — how Grandpa's catheter got stuck in his urethra and how the doctors had to cut it out.

Yep, that catheter story never fails to clear the dining room in five seconds flat.

It requires no effort to experience discomfort when listening to tales like these, but it takes a seasoned Superior to get riled enough to order your relatives to shut the hell up ... for the sake of the children, if nothing else.

MANDATORY WEDDING RITUALS LIKE CAKE-SMASHING, HANDCUFFS AND "HELP ME" WRITTEN ON THE SOLES OF THE GROOM'S SHOES.

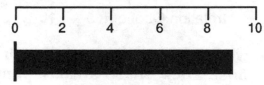

Irritation Quotient: 9

These examples call for outrage because they are part of what is supposed to be a meaningful celebration.

The bride and groom bashing pieces of cake in each other's face at the wedding reception is so stupid, no one even remembers why it's done. It just *is*, and that's apparently good enough to carry on the tradition.

Even more appalling is what transpires at some of your less classy wedding *services:* Namely, witnessing the groom kneeling, revealing that some hilarious jokester wrote the words "Help me" on the soles of his shoes, then watching the newlyweds exit the church with their hands joined together with a pair of white handcuffs.

If they want to use those cuffs later in the hotel room, that's one thing — but they have no business wearing them at the wedding.

As these low-lifes exit the church, in lieu of rice the congregation should toss ball-bearings.

PEOPLE WHO INSIST THEY HAVE TO LEAVE, THEN PROCEED TO HANG AROUND FOR AN HOUR OR MORE.

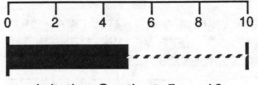

Irritation Quotient: 5 ↔ 10

People who come over to visit you, invited or not, can cause a few sharp anxiety pangs when they state they "really have to go," then proceed to hem and haw and talk some more.

This annoyance increases in intensity depending on how late in the evening it is and how much the people bother you to begin with. Generally, though, if it was *you* announcing it was time for *you* to go, and nobody jumped up begging you to stay, you would make your farewells and hit the road. So, when people say they're leaving, then hang out some more, and some more, and some more, this irritation can eventually reach a level where you *feel* like giving them a real good reason to leave — like, to go to the dentist to realign their front teeth!

* * *

Another part of being an SP is knowing when to sum things up and get on to the next book. So it's just about time for me to bid you adieu.

Besides, my first Inferior Person "fan" letter has just arrived and I can't wait to open it. Hmmm??? What's that ticking noise...

IN SUMMATION

Whew! Exhausted? You've just sped through over 200 varieties of common irritations which grate on Superior People's nerves. So, are you an SP? By now, you should have no doubt.

It is vital to remember that being Superior does *not* mean you're perfect or that you deserve special treatment (believe it or not).

What it does mean is that you know how to conduct yourself in a public or private place with a degree of class. It means you can easily recognize when other people are behaving like morons. It means that when you're right about something, you say so. Similarly, when you're wrong, you say so and when you're unsure, you say so.

Superiors know the therapeutic value of blaming inanimate objects for their own dumb errors and for irritations not directly caused by other people.

Superiors are independent thinkers, highly observant, quietly opinionated, always striving for self-improvement and are self-motivated. They possess a well-developed sense of humor, learn from their mistakes and enjoy watching other people. (Might as well throw in "incredibly modest" while we're at it.) Above all these things, they know themselves very well and are generally happy and self-satisfied folk (when not being irritated by Inferiors).

Finally, remember that being an SP is a bit of a "catch-22." You can't be annoyed to this extent *that* often without being a Superior Person with Superior Awareness, and you can't be a Superior Person with Superior Awareness without being super-sensitive to all these irritating realities. Both qualities go hand-in-hand, and there ain't no separatin' 'em. So, as an SP, prepare to be bugged.

But you can handle it, and after awhile you'll find that being irked can be loads of fun, so much so that you'll catch yourself actually *seeking out* sources of irritation. And this built-in entertainment value makes you look that much closer at the amazing human behavior that goes on all around you every day of the week.

Good luck with being the best Superior Person you can be. And remember to laugh. That really helps a lot.

HAVING COMPLETED
~THIS BOOK~

IS HEREBY GRANTED
SUPERIOR
PERSON
~STATUS~

OH, ABOUT THAT AUTHOR

Russ Lindway, a graduate of Baldwin-Wallace College in Berea, Ohio and self-convinced Superior Person, resides with his wife Jean and budgie George somewhere in Northeastern Ohio. A radio and television comedy writer since 1979, and an advertising creative-type since 1989, Lindway has amassed a whole two Emmy Awards and an Award for Cable Excellence (ACE) for his writing and producing work. He currently writes in an abandoned, unplugged refrigerator in his cellar. (Don't worry, he took the door off first.)

TITLES BY CCC PUBLICATIONS
—NEW BOOKS—
THE SUPERIOR PERSON'S GUIDE TO EVERYDAY IRRITATIONS

HOW TO TALK YOUR WAY OUT OF A TRAFFIC TICKET

YOUR GUIDE TO CORPORATE SURVIVAL

WHAT DO WE DO NOW?? (The Complete Guide For All New Parents Or Parents-To-Be)

—WINTER 1990 RELEASES—
GIFTING RIGHT (How To Give A Great Gift For Any Occasion Every Time)

HOW TO REALLY PARTY

HORMONES FROM HELL

SINGLE AND AVOIDING AIDS

—BEST SELLERS—
NO HANG-UPS (Funny Answering Machine Messages)

NO HANG-UPS II

NO HANG-UPS III

GETTING EVEN WITH THE ANSWERING MACHINE

HOW TO GET EVEN WITH YOUR EXes

HOW TO SUCCEED IN SINGLES BARS

TOTALLY OUTRAGEOUS BUMPER-SNICKERS

THE "MAGIC BOOKMARK" BOOK COVER [Accessory Item]

—CASSETTES—
NO HANG-UPS TAPES (Funny, Pre-recorded Answering Machine Messages With Hilarious *Sound Effects*) — In Male or Female Voices

Vol. I: GENERAL MESSAGES
Vol. II: BUSINESS MESSAGES
Vol. III: 'R' RATED
Vol. IV: SOUND EFFECTS ONLY

Coming Soon:
Vol. V: CELEBRI-TEASE (Celebrity Impersonations)
Vol. VI: MESSAGES FOR SPORTS FANS

P.S.

(PLEASE SEND)

Of course, these irritations only scratch the surface of the total amount of irksome things which prey on SPs' nerves. If you would care to share a personal irritation of your own which you think is funny or clever (and original), write it on the back of this page — or on a separate sheet of paper (if you are irritated by **PEOPLE WHO TEAR PAGES OUT OF BOOKS**) — and send your entry to:

"EVERYDAY IRRITATIONS"

c/o CCC Publications
20306 Tau Place
Chatsworth, CA 91311

If our Editorial Department likes your entry, you will receive a check for **$5.00**, plus **YOUR NAME** and **YOUR IRRITATION** will appear in THE SUPERIOR PERSON'S GUIDE TO EVERYDAY IRRITATIONS — Book II!

Approximately 50 irritation entries submitted by readers will be selected for *Book II*.

[NOTE: In the case of duplicate or similar entries, the entrant with the earliest postmark *only* shall receive cash and credit. Upon payment of $5.00, CCC Publications owns exclusive right of usage of the entry. *All* submissions become the property of CCC Publications and cannot be returned. Only the entries which appear in *Book II* shall receive cash and credit. Unused entries will be disposed of at CCC Publications' discretion. "PLEASE SEND" is subject to cancellation at anytime without notification.]

"EVERYDAY IRRITATIONS" ENTRY:

_____

_____

_____

_____

_____

_____

_____

_____

_____

_____

_____

SUBMITTED BY:

_____

NAME

_____

ADDRESS

_____

CITY   ZIP

_____

Phone # (Optional)